A REFUGE FROM THE STORM

A REFUGE FROM THE STORM

LAWRENCE MAXWELL

Pacific Press Publishing Association
Boise, Idaho
Oshawa, Ontario, Canada

Edited by Bonnie Widicker
Designed by Tim Larson
Cover photos by Harald Sund/The Image Bank©; Betty Blue
Type set in 10/12 Century Schoolbook

Library of Congress Catalog Number: 89-60218

ISBN 0-8163-0839-X

89 90 91 92 93 • 5 4 3 2 1

Contents

Chapter 1

Tornadoes on the Flight Path Home!

(Revelation 12:1-16)

God is our refuge and strength, a very present help in trouble. Psalm 46:1.

A storm had been blowing over America's central states all day. Walking across the concrete to change planes, I had seen its fury at one airport after another. Now waiting in Chicago for the final flight to Washington, I could feel the plane beneath me bounce and shake as if the wind would roll it across the field. Fully half an hour late, the pilot came aboard with ominous news.

"The weather people report possible tornadoes between here and Washington," he told us as he led his crew to the cockpit. "We're going up to see if we can find a way through."

Tornadoes on the flight path home! I looked around desperately for the nearest exit and thought momentarily of dashing for the door, shouting, "Let me out!" Then I remembered.

The captain had said, "We're going up." I had seen him lead his crew into the cockpit. He hadn't said, "Have a good flight! Hope you make it!" and then walked off the plane. *He was going with us.* How carefully he would guide the plane, if not for our sakes, then certainly for his own! Fear gave way to confidence. I relaxed, enjoyed watching the aurora borealis out the left-side windows, and in two or three hours arrived home, safe and sound.

Fearsome Storm Coming

How much that flight is like the book of Revelation! Here we read of catastrophes more deadly then tornadoes, of persecutions harsh enough to strike fear into the heart of the stoutest Christian. And the worst is ahead—on the flight path home, as it were. Already the stifling clouds of intolerance grow darker; the bitter winds of bigotry, more fierce.

Ellen White wrote, "The 'time of trouble, such as never was,' is soon to open upon us. . . . It is often the case that trouble is greater in anticipation than in reality; but this is not true of the crisis before us. The most vivid presentation cannot reach the magnitude of the ordeal" (*The Great Controversy,* p. 622).

But ringing like a silver bell above the shrieking wind, shining clearly in the darkness, echoing in the silence of a thousand dungeons, breaking through the smoke of a million martyr fires comes the lovely voice of Jesus: "I am with you. Hold on a little longer. Help is on the way. I will be your refuge in the storm. Soon you will be home, sitting with Me on My throne."

Nowhere else in the Bible are the woes of the Christian church so darkly portrayed as they are in Revelation; and nowhere else is the grand consummation of the church so gloriously revealed.

When Everything Goes Wrong

How much we need that encouragement when everything seems to go wrong for us! How much John needed it that Sabbath morning as he sat on a rock gazing at the imprisoning sea! Certainly everything seemed to have gone wrong for him.

It's not hard to imagine his thoughts. Surely his mind went back to those earlier, happy days when he and his brother James and their cousins Peter and Andrew caught fish in the sparkling waters of Galilee. How vigorous the young men had been then! So full of strength and hope and dreams! How excited they were to leave the lake and join John the Baptist by the Jordan—and see Jesus!

Then what brilliant prospects they had mapped out for themselves, sure that this Miracle Worker they walked with, who drew such vast, adoring crowds, was the promised Deliverer. John smiled ruefully as he remembered the endless quarrels with his friends as each claimed for himself the highest position in the new kingdom. Long before Patmos he had perceived that Jesus had never planned to establish His throne on earth back then. But what bitter experiences he had suffered to learn that lesson!

He knew he would never forget that dreadful weekend when Jesus was crucified and lay dead in the tomb. Or that memorable morning, six weeks later, when Jesus led the disciples to the top of Olivet. Even yet the hope had lingered that He might, even now, claim dominion over Rome. But it was not to be. While Jesus was talking, He had gone up into the sky, and a cloud had received Him out of their sight. Yet, even as their dreams crumbled around them, the disciples heard two angels assure them that this same Jesus would come again, just as they had seen Him go.

Bright New Hope

Inspired with new courage, the disciples had carefully reviewed their many conversations with Jesus. First and foremost, they remembered, He had told them to tell the world the good news about Himself. Then, they remembered, He had said, "When this gospel has been preached in all the world, I will return." Buoyed up with joy and hope, they had hurried to earth's remotest bounds, determined to preach the gospel to the world in the shortest possible time. And they had succeeded beyond their dreams. Even their enemies said they had turned the world upside down. There were new believers everywhere.

Then, why hadn't Jesus come? Actually, if Jesus didn't come soon, all their efforts might be lost. The other disciples had already passed away. James, John's brother, had been among the first to go. Peter had been crucified. Paul—not a disciple, to be sure, but such a tower of strength—had been beheaded outside Rome. Name them, one after another, all gone, except himself; and here he was, stuck on this island, where he couldn't preach if he tried. Sometimes, lately, he'd felt so weary. He'd be gone too, soon, and then what would happen to the believers?

It was twenty-five years now since Jerusalem was destroyed and the temple razed—just as Jesus had said they would be. The believers had always looked to Jerusalem for leadership, for that was where the leaders lived. But not anymore, not with Jerusalem gone. There was no central city or church or group anywhere that the Christians could rally around. And the churches! What deplorable condition they were in!

John thought of the seven he knew best. The Laodiceans had become so enthralled by makeup and clothing and money, and so lukewarm about spiritual things, there didn't seem much hope for them any more. And Sardis! The only word to describe Sardis was *dead*. Oh, there were a few faithful left, but so few. And his own beloved Ephesians! They had let their first love die, and nothing availed to revive it.

Why didn't Jesus come? Had He forsaken them? Or, worse yet, amid all the glories of heaven, had He—dreadful thought—had He forgotten them?

The Voice of a Friend

Surely it was at some such unhappy point in John's brooding that a voice like a trumpet startled him. He turned and saw his dear Friend, Jesus, standing behind him.

Forgotten? Not at all! Jesus proceeded to give John messages for the seven churches that proved beyond a doubt that He remembered them well. He mentioned weaknesses, and He listed many a strong point that John, in his despondence, had overlooked. Beyond that, He made such promises to each church as must surely cheer them on to do their best for their Saviour.

After that first vision, Jesus had given John another, of a scroll with seven seals and what happened when the seals were opened; and then a third, of angels holding seven trumpets and what happened when the angels blew them. Each vision showed, with increasing detail, that Jesus knew all that was happening to the Christians—and all that was going to happen to them and to the nations around them till the end of time, when He would come and gather the faithful into His kingdom above.

What comfort those visions must have brought the lonely disciple. Undoubtedly he hoped Jesus would tell him more. He was not disappointed. Soon Jesus returned to give John another vision, one of great significance to us living today.

The "Great Controversy Vision"

The fourth vision, which we find in Revelation 12 to 14, is one of the most comprehensive in the Bible. It stretches over a longer period of time than any other. And in no other is the great controversy between Christ and Satan so clearly described.

This "great controversy vision," as we may call it, began like the first three—with a brief view into the heavenly temple. It must have given John a sense of great assurance to know that, though the old temple was gone, there was still a temple in heaven, infinitely more glorious than the one he had admired so much on earth, and that his Friend, Jesus, ministered for him there.

Unlike the first three temple scenes, which focused on the Holy Place, this one took John into the Holy of Holies. (Look in the last verse of chapter 11.) John saw the ark containing the Ten Commandments. If he wondered whether this new vision would deal extensively with the commandments and the final judgment, he was right.

Lovely Mother, Angry Dragon

To the accompaniment of lightning, thunder, and hail, the heavenly temple faded. Before John's wondering eyes appeared a beautiful woman about to bear a child, and a dragon standing nearby, ready to devour the baby as soon as it was born. The mother gave birth to a boy, and the dragon lunged for him; but the child was caught safely up to heaven, and the frustrated dragon attacked the woman.

John must have recognized many events of this scene. He had participated in them, especially the day when the Boy, grown up, had stood on the Mount of Olives and was "caught up" into heaven. He knew personally about the attack on the woman. It was religious persecution that had brought him here to Patmos.

Again the scene changed, in a manner so typical of Revelation and so confusing to its readers. It helps to have watched the Olympics on television! Viewers of the games soon get acquainted with the networks' habit of picking a winner ahead of time and interviewing him or her long before the games begin. Then, when that athlete's contest is announced and the viewers have seen him or her compete in some early heats, the networks interrupt their coverage to run their interview, giving viewers insights into the athlete's background and ambitions. The program returns to current events, and the contests continue till the chosen athlete wins or loses. So, here.

The opening scene had introduced the dragon and showed his unsuccessful attempt to kill the baby Jesus back during the time just before John was born. The second scene—the "interview"—showed that the dragon had determined to destroy Christ long before that, way back before the beginning of time. He had actually waged war on Jesus in heaven. Jesus had mobilized the faithful angels to drive him and his cohorts out. Now, unable to attack Jesus personally, the deported demons were working out their venomous rage upon Christ's faithful followers on earth.

It was a significant revelation. It made the saints' sufferings so much more meaningful. It was not just Herod who had tried to kill the baby Jesus or Pilate who had crucified Him; neither was it simply Nero who had beheaded Paul or Domitian who had exiled John. Behind these evil men, working through them, was the devil himself. And the reason he attacked faithful Christians was that they were the nearest beings to Christ that he could reach.

What honor, then, to be a target of persecution! Satan sees that his victims have characters so like the character of Christ, that attacking them is almost the same as attacking Jesus.

Defeated, but Still Living

Many must have asked John, as millions have asked their

ministers since, "Why, instead of merely driving Satan out of heaven, didn't God destroy him and put an end to sin at once?" The answer is that destroying Satan would have struck fear into the hearts of the angels. God doesn't want them to serve Him because they are afraid of Him, but because they love Him. The service of fear produces rebellion.

Another question John may have been asked is, "Why didn't God, in a nanosecond of time, vaporize the devil and all the angels, good and bad, and start over? That way, no one would know what happened, and none would be afraid." To this question there are two answers. First, God doesn't do things that way. And second, He wanted the angels to know.

God Wants Us to Know

He wants us all to know about Satan and where his ideas lead, and He wants us to know all about Himself. He wants us to know that He isn't kind and generous and loving only when He is obeyed and adored—as Satan charged. He wants us to know that He is loving whatever happens. Slice a marshmallow. Any way you cut it, you get only marshmallow; because a marshmallow is *marshmallow*. Cut a well-baked loaf of bread into thin slices or thick, dice it, crumb it, test it as you may, all you will get is bread; because a loaf of bread is *bread.* So with God. Seat Him on His throne, adore Him, praise Him, obey Him, and His response is love. Or place Him under the cruel power of Satan, insult Him, bruise Him, drive nails into His hands and feet and stand back and taunt Him, and His response is love; because *God is love.*

God wants the whole universe, sooner or later, to know this about Him. It is necessary for all to see the malicious results of evil, so that all can choose God or His adversary on the basis of evidence. Only thus will heaven's future be secure.

The war having begun, God is determined to let it go on to its natural conclusion. He doesn't want to go through any part of it again.

Persecuted, but Sheltered

Chapter 12, verse 13 says that "the dragon . . . persecuted

the woman," and she fled into the wilderness. Verse 15 says that the "serpent cast out . . . a flood after the woman," and the earth swallowed it. Whether these two expressions describe one event, in the manner of Hebrew poetry, or two succeeding events is hard to say. But, in fact, there were two phases to the persecution.

During the first nine centuries after 538, peasants were too ignorant of the Scriptures and too frightened by churchly power to propose very many new religious ideas. Those who dared to believe differently were persecuted, but the wilderness areas of largely uninhabited Europe were broad enough to afford them considerable protection.

In the late fifteenth century, some scholars came from the East and taught a few European students how to translate the original Bible languages. Luther in Germany and Tyndale in England grasped the opportunity. After 1522 and 1525, Bibles in German and English rapidly became the common property of ordinary folk. The Reformation, which had just begun, exploded! The towering bulwarks of the medieval church shook to their foundations. Hell was aroused as never before in history. For the rest of that century and all through the next, the forces of intolerance hurled floods of malicious fury at the Reformed churches, hoping to destroy them forever.

In the midst of this vicious storm, God provided a refuge. At this very time (around 1620), the forested shores beyond the Atlantic opened their arms to shelter the beleaguered targets of the dragon's wrath, just as God had promised.

The vision was still scarcely begun. Already John had seen enough to know that the persecution would be more intense and last far longer than he had imagined. He had also seen that through it all God would ever be close to His people, sustaining them, encouraging them, and never failing to provide a safe refuge in the storm.

Chapter 2

"His Treasured Possession"

(Revelation 12:17)

The dragon was wroth with the woman, and went to make war with the remnant of her seed, which keep the commandments of God, and have the testimony of Jesus Christ. Revelation 12:17.

From the very beginning, God has wanted a people on earth upon whom He could pour His richest blessings; men and women so holy, so obedient to His commandments and respectful of His counsel that upon them and through them He could demonstrate to the universe the exceeding riches of His grace.

When He made the world, He made it "very good." Then He went further. Planting "a garden eastward in Eden," He placed there the very choicest of His gifts and gave them to Adam and Eve to enjoy through all future time.

Alas, the entrance of sin spoiled that generous plan. The warfare that had begun in heaven was transferred to earth, and the forces of good and evil arrayed themselves to battle for the lives and souls of men.

The early families that followed Adam and Eve failed to live up to God's high hopes. They became more and more corrupt until every thought of their hearts was only evil continually. Violence so filled the land that God had to destroy all but eight in the Flood.

Brand New Opportunity

When the cleansing waters receded, a great new opportunity opened for Noah and his children. Their descendants could be those holy, obedient, loving people God wanted so much to bless.

But again, it was not to be. Quicker than the first time, degeneracy set in once more. Soon vice and corruption were rampant. Oppression and bloodshed spread terror everywhere. Idol worship of the most debasing kind almost obliterated knowledge of the true God. As the centuries passed, the soil was littered with the bodies of multiplied millions of wrecked and ruined lives.

Yet through it all God was never without witnesses. Through even the most discouraging times there were always a few noble souls who remained true to Him. Though the darkness of sin settled over the land, the light of God's love never totally went out. There were always a few to pass along the message of His goodness and grace.

One of these faithful few was Abraham. God was so pleased with him that He offered to make of his family a great nation through whom He would bless the world. When famine threatened to destroy Abraham's descendants, God preserved them in Egypt whence, after a while, He led them out, through the desert, to a land that would be wholly their own. There, free from heathen oppression and totally at liberty to follow God, they could develop those holy, obedient characters God could so abundantly bless.

High Hopes for Israel

To make sure there would be no disappointment this time, God instructed Moses to tell the Israelites just what kind of people He wanted them to be. They were to make no covenant with the wicked inhabitants of the land, they were not to marry their sons and daughters to the children of the unconverted, and they were to break down the heathens' altars and burn their idols. Then Moses explained why God wanted this. "You are a people holy to the Lord your God," he told the Israelites. "The Lord your God has chosen you out of all the oples on the face of the earth to be his people, his treasured possession. The Lord did not set his affection on you and choose you because you were more numerous than other peoples, for you were the fewest of all peoples. But it was because the Lord loved you and kept the oath he swore to your forefathers. . . . Therefore, take care to follow the commands, decrees and laws I give you today. . . . He will love you and bless you and increase your numbers. . . . You will be blessed more than any other people" (Deuteronomy 5:6-14, NIV).

"His treasured possession." What an honor. What a privilege. Could anyone lightly turn it down?

To make doubly sure Israel understood their opportunity, Moses spoke to them again. "Behold, I have taught you statutes and judgments, even as the Lord my God commanded me, that ye should do so in the land whither ye go to possess it. Keep therefore and do them; for this is your wisdom and your understanding in the sight of the nations, which shall hear all these statutes, and say, Surely this great nation is a wise and understanding people. For what nation is there so great who hath God so nigh unto them?" (Deuteronomy 4:5-7).

The voice was the voice of Moses, but the words were the words of God. We can almost hear God's voice break with emotion as He pleads, "Please, be My people. Do what I command you, listen to what My prophets tell you, because I want so much to bless you. I have been unjustly criticized and falsely accused. Let Me demonstrate through you what a happy, healthy, prosperous people is that nation whose God is the Lord."

If only Israel had appreciated God's offer, how different the course of history would have been!

Disappointed Again

Israel, as a nation, let God down. To be sure, in the years that followed the entry into the Promised Land, there were a few bursts of piety now and then; but the general trend was downward, till Israel deserved Isaiah's stern rebuke:

"Ah sinful nation, a people laden with iniquity, a seed of evildoers, children that are corrupters: they have forsaken the

Lord, they have provoked the Holy One of Israel unto anger, they are gone away backward. . . . The whole head is sick, and the whole heart faint. From the sole of the foot even unto the head there is no soundness in it; but wounds, and bruises, and putrefying sores" (Isaiah 1:4-6).

Yet God's patience was still unexhausted. He had Isaiah tell the inhabitants of Jerusalem: "Wash you, make you clean; put away the evil of your doings from before mine eyes; cease to do evil; learn to do well. . . . Come now, and let us reason together, saith the Lord: though your sins be as scarlet, they shall be as white as snow; though they be red like crimson, they shall be as wool. If ye be willing and obedient, ye shall eat the good of the land" (Isaiah 1:16-19).

Then Isaiah pointed out one thing the people must do. "If thou turn away thy foot from the sabbath, from doing thy pleasure on my holy day; and call the sabbath a delight, the holy of the Lord, honourable; and shalt honour him, not doing thine own ways, nor finding thine own pleasure, nor speaking thine own words: then shalt thou delight thyself in the Lord; and I will cause thee to ride upon the high places of the earth" (Isaiah 58:13, 14).

Even now God stood ready, willing, eager to bless them. Indeed, to make theirs the greatest nation on earth.

But Israel did not respond; it was almost as if God had not spoken. Again and again He called. "The Lord God of their fathers sent to them by his messengers, rising up betimes, and sending; because he had compassion on his people, and on his dwelling place: but they mocked the messengers of God, and despised his words, and misused his prophets" (2 Chronicles 36:15, 16). "Last of all he sent unto them his son, saying, They will reverence my son" (Matthew 21:37).

God in the person of Jesus walked the dusty streets His people walked, ate their food, dressed in their clothes. He healed their sick, comforted their sorrowing, encouraged their depressed, even raised their dead to life and forgave their sins. When they said to Him, "Show us the Father," He replied, "If you have seen Me, you have seen the Father" (see John 14:8, 9).

But His ways were not their ways. Their grasping greed

grated against His generous spirit. His willingness to forgive rebuked their demands for retribution. His concept of a master who served was alien to their dreams of a deliverer who would destroy their enemies. And because Jesus' representation of God was so different from their own, they rejected Him. To all their other sins, they added this crowning folly: they crucified Him. The hammer that drove the nails through Jesus' hands and feet tolled the knell of Israel's special relationship with God.

Though the nation as a whole had rejected Him, a few, a remnant, loved Him enough to obey His commandments and trust His word. He could work through them. They would be the channels through whom He would yet bless the world.

Another New Start

Within hours of the Resurrection there was a growing group that believed. Within a week, as Passover ended, hundreds were hurrying to their homes in distant places, bearing the good news. Pentecost was not over before thousands had accepted God's invitation.

The Crucifixion had accomplished what fifteen hundred years of preaching had failed to achieve. God now had a band of thousands of believers personally committed to live as He lived, to love as He loved, and to tell everyone they could reach about the exceeding riches of His grace. Moreover, this was no longer a national movement. The cry was heard, "We turn to the Gentiles," and soon intrepid Christians, their hearts burning with new-kindled love, were venturing to the farthest boundaries of the Roman Empire—and beyond. Before the first century was out, scarcely a city or village remained that had not heard the message of God's goodness or been offered the thrilling invitation to taste His mercy.

Persecution seemed only to spur the messengers on and to keep their teaching pure. But in time the cunning malice of the dragon changed all that. The attitude of government authorities modulated from persecution to patronage. Superstitions and outright heathen ceremonies suddenly swept into the church. The last mangled bodies of the martyrs were hardly buried before church doors were flung open to welcome the unconverted and insincere. Church rolls increased, but Christian belief and practice declined. Heartfelt prayers to the lovely Jesus and His gracious Father were replaced by recitations to dead saints. The simplicity of the gospel was confused by man-made dogmas without scriptural foundation.

Then persecution broke out afresh, this time sponsored by the church against those few who still remained faithful to Jesus. For, yes, there still were a few, holding Christ's banner high, keeping the light burning. Many were in dungeons or in mountain fastnesses or perhaps in distant lands where the cruel arm of the church could not reach them.

And, wonder of wonders, God showed John in this "great controversy vision" that after 1260 years of history's most cruel and determined persecution, there would still be a remnant, loving Jesus enough to keep His commandments and trusting Him enough to believe His testimony, even the special testimony God would send them through His latter-day prophet.

The Remnant at the Close

Seventh-day Adventists have little trouble demonstrating conclusively that the Seventh-day Adventist denomination is the remnant church. We arose as an organization after 1798, when the 1260 years of persecution were officially over. We teach that all God's commandments should be obeyed, including the fourth that requires Sabbath observance. We preach the three angels' messages. Unique among Christians, we proclaim that the investigative phase of the final judgment is already in session. We sponsor a worldwide work announcing that Christ is coming soon. And we have on our bookshelves the voluminous writings of Ellen G. White, God's latter-day prophet who gave us "the testimony of Jesus." It's all so easy to prove. The Seventh-day Adventist denomination is without doubt God's remnant church. A person who is a member of the Seventh-day Adventist Church is a member of God's remnant church. It's so incontestably correct. And important.

But much more important, and in many ways more difficult to answer—because it is so personal—is the question, "Am I a member of the remnant?" Paul made it clear that "they are not all Israel, which are of Israel: neither, because they are the seed of Abraham, are they all children. . . . The children of the promise," he said, "are counted for the seed" (Romans 9:6-8).

So to answer the question carelessly, to assume that because we are members of the remnant church we are automatically members of the remnant, is to run the risk of sharing the disappointment of the foolish virgins, the one-talent servant, and the goats. For, remember, the first were friends of the Bridegroom, the second was a servant of the Master, and the third were all members of the Shepherd's flock. Yet none entered the joy of the Lord. They were members of the remnant church, as it were, but not members of the remnant.

The best time to ask ourselves the question is now. Better yet, because our hearts are deceitful, ask Jesus for His answer. If we are already members of the remnant, He'll reassure us. If not, He will tell us gently what we need.

Failing to belong to the remnant, we may escape some of the dragon's wrath. But belonging makes us God's "treasured possession," members of that special group the Lord will so bountifully bless all through eternity. And we can be very sure He will be our refuge in the coming storm.

Chapter 3

Amazing Prophecies Accurately Fulfilled

(Revelation 13:1-10)

I saw one of his heads as it were wounded to death; and his deadly wound was healed: and all the world wondered after the beast. Revelation 13:3.

God never intended that His people should be fearful of the future, forever wondering what was going to happen next. He knows the end from the beginning, and He wants us to know too.

But we limit God. The human mind is capable of accepting only so much new material at one time (see John 16:12). When God wanted to tell Daniel all about the blasphemous little horn that grew up among the ten horns on a fourth beast (following the lion, the four-headed leopard, and the bear), Daniel was "troubled" in his mind. The strain showed on his face (see Daniel 7:28). In mercy, God cut the vision short. It would be more than 600 years before He returned to finish it.

Still, in the "great controversy vision," John doesn't tell us his personal reaction when he saw an animal with seven heads and ten horns coming out of the water. In all his years on Galilee, his nets had never brought up a creature remotely like it.

But he soon recognized that its ugly heads and horns grew out of a leopard's body with a lion's mouth and a bear's feet. Here were all the beasts and horns of Daniel 7 combined in one animal!

God had brought the dreadful beast on stage to give us some amazing news He hadn't given Daniel. That this great brute of a bully, which for 1260 years would conquer and crush all who challenged it, would be struck in the head with a deadly wound. And that this would happen just when the dragon began his angry attack on God's "treasured possession," the loyal remnant.

1260 Days

To be absolutely sure we would recognize this beast as the same one Daniel saw, John saw that it would blaspheme God and make war with the saints for "forty and two months" (see Revelation 13:5, 6). The little horn on Daniel's beast was to blaspheme God and wear out the saints for "a time and times and the dividing of time" (Daniel 7:25). With 30 days in a month, 42 months equals 1260 days. "A time" is a year with twelve months. A time plus two times plus half a time is 12 months plus 24 months plus 6 months, which also equals 42 months or 1260 days. Add them like this:

1 time	12 months	360 days
2 times	24 months	720 days
1/2 time	6 months	180 days
Total: 3 1/2 times	42 months	1260 days

One thousand two hundred and sixty days. The number sounds familiar. Of course! Just a few minutes ago, John learned that the persecuted church was to be fed in the wilderness "a thousand two hundred and threescore days" (Revelation 12:6). Moments after that, he was told that the church would be nourished in the wilderness "for a time, and times, and half a time" (verse 14).

Why is the same time period mentioned so often? In the trumpet vision—the one right before this "great controversy vision"—John was told that the Gentiles would tread on the holy city "forty and two months" and that God's two witnesses would prophesy in sackcloth "a thousand two hundred and threescore days" (Revelation 11:2, 3).

Three times in one vision, five times in two visions! God must consider the 1260-day period highly significant. Why?

One reason, no doubt, is that by repeating the time, He helped us identify the people and powers who participated in the long period of persecution.

Another reason for mentioning the number so often may have been to correct the mistaken idea, rampant among the believers of that time, that Jesus was coming back right away. Paul had to wrestle with the concept in the Thessalonian church. "We beseech you, brethren," he wrote, " . . . that ye be not soon shaken in mind, . . . as that the day of Christ is at hand. Let no man deceive you by any means: for that day shall not come, except there come a falling away first, and that man of sin be revealed, the son of perdition" (2 Thessalonians 2:1-3).

Jesus had tried to abort the problem. On the Tuesday night before He died, He told the disciples that there would be a long period of persecution before He returned. He urged the disciples to study Daniel to learn more about it (see Matthew 24:15, 21). In Daniel, the disciples would have found the 1260-day/year prophecy. In spite of Jesus' warning, the idea that Jesus was coming right away spread widely. If it had not been stopped, it could have wrecked the Christian church almost before it started; Jesus' failure to return as expected would have seriously undermined faith.

Because, in prophecy, a day stands for a year, the 1260-day prophecy warned the early believers to settle in for a long period of persecution; Christ's return was far in the future. To us, however, living on the other side of the persecution, the 1260 days shout, "Get ready, and be quick about it! Jesus is near, even at the door!"

Not Repeatable

Although 1260 days is referred to seven times in the Bible, the Bible does not predict seven 1260-year periods of persecution. That would require 8820 years and put off the second coming for another six millenniums at least. Some "signs" the Adventist often point to, like wars and earthquakes, famines and pestilences, false Christs and false prophets, are repeatable; but precisely because they are repeatable, they may not be very exact. Jesus listed them for the disciples and said, "The end is not yet." He went further. He said, "All these are the *beginning* of sorrows" (Matthew 24:6-8, emphasis supplied). The fact is that as long as we are in this world, there will be pain and pestilence, wars and famines and earthquakes, and many false guides to lead people astray. They are "par for the course" in this sinful world. They will continue till Jesus comes.

But the 1260 day/years (like the 2300 day/years) are not repeatable. Through Daniel, God gave explicit directions for identifying the start of the 1260 days. They would begin:

1. After Rome fell, divided into ten kingdoms. (Fulfilled A.D. 476.)
2. After three of the kingdoms were uprooted. (Fulfilled A.D. 492, 534, 538.)
3. When a religious power attempted to change God's law. (Fulfilled A.D. 538.)

History records that Rome fell in A.D. 476, divided among ten kingdoms. In the next sixty-two years, three of the ten were destroyed: the Heruls, Vandals, and Ostrogoths. Immediately after this, the Bishop of Rome chaired a church council in Orleans, near Paris, which passed a resolution requiring farmers not to work on Sunday but to go to church instead—even though God's commandment said all should work on Sunday and go to church on Saturday. This power had actually thought to change God's law! The year of the decree was 538. The 1260 day/years had begun! No similar combination of events can be found in all history (see C. Mervyn Maxwell, *God Cares*, vol. 1, p. 135).

Christ's Credibility on the Line

With 538 marking the commencement, adding 1260 years puts the end in 1798. To confirm this date, the Bible gives us three indicators. One, in Revelation, is the deadly wound. The other two were given by Jesus. He told His disciples, "Except those days [of persecution] should be shortened, there should no flesh be saved: but for the elect's sake those days shall be shortened" (Matthew 24:22). Then He made a prophecy that is absolutely amazing because it is so very specific. He put His credibility on the line; only a prophet with His foreknowledge would dare be so precise. He said, "In those days, after that [persecution], the sun shall be darkened, and the moon shall not give her light" (Mark 13:24). Let's recap these criteria:

1. End of persecution. (Fulfilled A.D. 1773.)
2. Dark day and night. (Fulfilled May 18/19, 1780.)
3. Deadly wound. (Fulfilled A.D. 1798.)

Historians tell us that the persecution was over by 1773, when Pope Clement XIV outlawed the Jesuits. The deadly wound was administered when Pope Pius VI was taken prisoner in 1798. This leaves a twenty-five year window, 1773 to 1798, in which the sun and moon must be darkened if we are to trust Jesus' prophecy. Now note this remarkable fact. The dark day and night occurred on May 18/19, 1780, neatly inside the narrow time slot Jesus had allowed for them. What an amazing fulfillment! Jesus proved His reliability. And the three indicators point precisely to 1798 as the end of the 1260 day/years.

That's why the 1260-day period is unrepeatable. We have looked at six historic events that came together exactly as predicted to establish its beginning and end. Search the long annals of history as we may, no similar set of events can be found anywhere else. Clearly then, 538 to 1798 are the dates for the fulfillment of the 1260-day prophecy, and no other period will do.

And that is just one of many reasons why Seventh-day Adventists can teach the nearness of the second advent with utmost confidence.

Wounded . . . and Partially Healed

Because Revelation 13:14 says the deadly wound was to be

made by a sword, the prophecy was appropriately fulfilled when a French army officer arrested Pope Pius VI as that elderly gentlemen (he was in his eighties) celebrated mass in the Sistine Chapel, with Michelangelo's famous pictures looking down from the ceiling.

Prophecy also said that the wound would be healed. Nearly 200 years have passed since 1798. The wound is healing, but it is far from completely well.

Adventists have traditionally associated the healing with various government actions, like the return of territory to the Vatican in 1929. The personal popularity of the present pope has contributed a great deal. But we must not overlook other factors, some of which may be more important.

For instance, one significant factor *slowing* the healing process has been the biblical faith and vigorous evangelizing of Protestantism. This was especially true in the early nineteenth century, when the Catholic Church was weaker. In just sixty years, membership in the Methodist Church in the United States leaped from less than 5,000 in 1800 to more than 2,000,000 in 1860. In those same decades, Protestants as a group built nearly 52,000 churches with a seating capacity above 18,000,000.

These zealous church builders knew they didn't have anywhere near enough members to fill their pews, and they fully intended to keep on evangelizing till they did. There just wasn't much room in the U.S.A. in those days for non-Protestants to operate! We'll take a closer look at this Protestant vigor in chapter 7.

If Protestant faith and vigor slowed the healing of the wound, then Protestant indifference might be expected to hasten it—especially if the Protestant malaise were accompanied by a revival of self-confidence among Catholics. We see this happening today, and we must be alert to it.

Ellen White's Credibility on the Line

In *The Great Controversy*, on page 579, Ellen White applies the deadly wound to the "downfall of the papacy in 1798." On page 581 she applies the healing of the wound to the "triumph of Rome" in the near future.

In light of the popularity of Pope John Paul II and the influence of his church today, it is easy to read Ellen White's prediction and say, "Of course. Everyone knows the prophecy refers to the Catholic Church." But we must remember that *The Great Controversy* was published in 1888, not 1989. A hundred years ago, everyone in the Christian world who knew anything about the Catholic Church knew that it was flat on its back and that it would never amount to much again.

For example, another highly respected Christian writer, Methodist Bible commentator Adam Clarke, writing in 1832, said that the Catholic Church in his day was "fast declining." He admitted that he couldn't understand Revelation and relied on another author to explain the deadly wound. This author said that the wound referred to the fall of Rome in 476 and the healing to an act of Charlemagne around the year 800 (see Adam Clarke, *Commentary*, vol. 6, pp. 962, 966, 1017, 1018). How wrong he was!

As recently as 1975, the Anchor Bible came out with another interpretation. Calling on all the wisdom and research of modern scholarship, the author of the volume on Revelation suggests that the wound may have occurred when the emperor Nero became angry with Vespasian for falling asleep during his musical performances and exiled Vespasian from Rome. The healing, according to this commentator, occurred when Vespasian was called back to fight for the empire against the Jews in Judea (see J. Massynberde Ford, *Revelation*, vol. 38 in William Foxwell Albright and David Noel Freedman, eds., *The Anchor Bible* [Garden City, New York: Doubleday & Company, 1975], page 221). How wrong he was!

Unique among Bible commentators, Ellen White interpreted the prophecy correctly. Let's give her credit.

God's Credibility on the Line

So much of Revelation 13 describes the baneful successes of the beast that it seems at first reading to predict total victory for the forces of evil. But read the chapter again. One sentence—actually it's only part of a sentence—shines out with the brilliance of the evening star. Verse 8 says that everyone on earth will worship the beast "whose names are not written in the book of life of the Lamb slain from the foundation of the world."

Wonderful thought! *Not* everyone on earth will worship the beast. In spite of threats and imprisonment, in spite of scourging and martyrdom, no matter how fiercely the gale tears at their faith, some will remain loyal to God, and God will write their names in the Lamb's book of life.

How do we know? Because God tells us.

But how does God know? Because He has faith in human beings.

What a beautiful thought! God, who has never let anyone down, asks us to trust Him, and we question whether it's really safe to do so. We make conditions and demand assurances. Meanwhile God, who knows how many times human beings have let Him down, still has confidence in us. He still believes that some will be true and faithful though all the dread forces of the dragon are assailed against them. And He doesn't mind saying so. He's even put it in the Bible for all to read. He has put His credibility on the line.

Can we do less than prove Him right?

Can we doubt that those who do so will find Him a refuge when the storm of persecution breaks out again?

Chapter 4

A Day to Fall in Love

(Revelation 13:11-18)

He had power to . . . cause that as many as would not worship the image of the beast should be killed. . . . And that no man might buy or sell, save he that had the mark, or the name of the beast, or the number of his name. Revelation 13:15-17.

It is night time, close to midnight. The frightened family huddles in the living room, lights out, doors locked. The baby sleeps fitfully, held tight in mother's arms. Two older children, a boy and a girl, cling to their parents. Then the dread sounds are heard: a truck stopping in front, heavy boots on the porch, rifle butts pounding the door. Police break in. After a brief scuffle, the truck drives off, leaving the front door gaping for early morning looters, and taking the family to certain death in the gas chambers of a concentration camp.

That is the World War II version of religious intolerance; and its constant rehearsal, in books and magazines, over radio and television, on stage and in schools, serves to keep a widely scattered ethnic group united.

The Adventist Version

Adventists have a slightly different version, based on Revelation 13:8-11. In ours, the tense family keeps a close, apprehensive watch on the daily news. The car is crammed with camping equipment, dried food, and as much warm clothing as can be squeezed in; the gas tank is kept full. Table conversation concentrates on God's promises of deliverance and the hope of the second coming. Bibles lie open on the furniture, easily available for memorizing promises of God's protection (especially Psalm 91) and accessible for picking up quickly at the last moment.

At family worships, Dad reads the final chapters of *The Great Controversy*. Family food stocks are low, partly because food has been difficult to obtain from hostile storekeepers and partly because Dad has been laid off; his company discovered that he still kept Saturday for the Sabbath. Once-friendly neighbors have taken to scrawling insults and threats on outside doors and walls.

Then, this evening, as the family watches, comes the dread news. The announcer reports that Congress today passed a national Sunday law with the death penalty for noncompliance; the President is expected to approve. All eyes turn to Dad. He whispers, "This is the sign," and offers a short prayer that all will remain faithful. Mother says, "You children know what to do. Gather your things and get into the car. Don't forget your Bibles." The teenage daughter says, "We'd better tell Mrs. Wilkinson," and reaches for the phone. Mother is heavy-hearted, because the oldest son has chosen to throw in his lot with the world; but the family is glad that one of the neighbors has been taking Bible studies and has expressed a sincere desire to join God's remnant. Soon the car is driving through familiar streets for the last time. At the edge of town, Dad turns the front wheels toward the mountains.

Mountains or Dungeons?

There are variations on this version, of course; but all include a national Sunday law and the death penalty. And they all have Adventists fleeing to the mountains in harmony with *The Great Controversy*, page 626: "The people of God will flee from the cities and villages and associate together in companies, dwelling in the most desolate and solitary places. Many will find refuge in the strongholds of the mountains."

All the variations, it seems, overlook a later sentence in the same paragraph: "Many of all nations and of all classes, high and low, rich and poor, black and white, will be cast into the most unjust and cruel bondage. The beloved of God pass weary days, bound in chains, shut in by prison bars, sentenced to be slain, some apparently left to die of starvation in dark and loathsome dungeons." Is it possible that more will be in bondage, chains, prisons, and dungeons than will manage to escape to the mountains? Will that World War II scene we considered first apply to more Adventists than we want to think?

To a certain extent, the persecution theme does for Adventists what it did for victims of Nazi intolerance; it gives the church a shared experience of suffering that tends to hold it together. No doubt this is healthy to a degree. But how many would-be church members has it frightened away? How many students in our academies choose to follow the ways of the world rather than risk the dreadful sufferings depicted by well-meaning Bible teachers and week of prayer speakers whose intent is to challenge, not terrify? Because the Bible says persecution is coming, we need to teach the youth about it. And because persecution is always frightening, we may need to place much more emphasis than we have on the sustaining and protecting power of God. We must assure everyone that God will be a refuge to His people in the storm.

Mark and Seal

Just how John, in the "great controversy vision," learned that the lamblike beast had power to slay all who would not worship the image of the beast or receive its mark, we are not told. And John does not tell us that the mark of the beast is Sunday keeping or that the seal of God is Sabbath keeping. These important interpretations were developed through much prayer and Bible study by Adventist pioneers and were confirmed by messages from God through Ellen White.

To say that the seal of God is Sabbath keeping raises two questions of such very great importance that every Adventist will want to answer them personally.

The first is, What kind of Sabbath keeping wins the seal of God? We have evidence that one can be a lifelong Sabbath keeper and never receive God's seal.

Sabbath Keepers Who Failed

The Jews of 2,000 years ago were strict Sabbath keepers. In many ways they were indistinguishable from modern Seventh-day Adventists. They paid a faithful tithe. They scrupulously observed a health-reform diet. They studied the Bible daily. They supported church schools and enrolled their children in them. They prayed long prayers and sang God-centered hymns. They looked for the coming of Christ and spoke about it eagerly. And on the Friday afternoon when they crucified Christ, they hurried home before sunset to keep the Sabbath.

For them, Sabbath keeping was not the seal of God. One might even say that for some of them the Sabbath of crucifixion weekend sealed forever their separation from God.

But they thought they kept the Sabbath. And they observed all those other right and proper duties. What important element was missing from their Sabbath keeping? Faithful Seventh-day Adventists today will certainly want the right answer to that question, lest the heavenly watchers see the same lack in our Sabbath keeping.

In view of the prophecy that Sabbath keepers are to be fined, hassled, even killed for keeping Sabbath, the other important question every Adventist will want to give careful study to is, Is my Sabbath worth dying for?

Sabbaths Worth Dying For

An Adventist businessman who has since become quite wealthy asked his pastor to remove his name from the church rolls because he was standing in the bank one day, waiting to make a deposit, when he suddenly realized it was Sabbath morning. "My business has crowded the Sabbath out of my life," he said. Apparently his Sabbaths were not worth losing money over. Friends still pray for him.

Through the prophet Isaiah, God promised the Israelites that if they would keep the Sabbath right, it would be a joyful day, worth any imaginable cost. " 'If you keep your feet from breaking the Sabbath and from doing as you please on my holy day,' " He said, " 'if you call the Sabbath a delight and the

Lord's holy day honorable, and if you honor it by not going your own way and not doing as you please or speaking idle words, then you will find your joy in the Lord, and I will cause you to ride on the heights of the land and to feast on the inheritance of your father Jacob' " (Isaiah 58:13, 14, NIV).

Good-enough-to-die-for Sabbath keeping means observing the Sabbath from sundown to sundown (see Mark 1:32). It includes shutting the gates of our homes and minds at Friday sunset against every kind of worldly business and interest, and keeping them shut the full twenty-four hours—as Nehemiah shut the gates of Jerusalem against the vendors who wanted to bring in all sorts of merchandise to sell on holy time (see Nehemiah 13:15-21). Many Adventists have family worship at the beginning and end of Sabbath, with Bible reading and hymns and prayer. It's a good custom for all Adventists to adopt.

Sabbath keeping that brings the seal of God includes going to God's house to study the Bible and worship God every Sabbath morning, as Jesus always did (see Luke 4:16). It includes all-of-the-family activities in the afternoon, for the children are not in school then, and Mom and Dad don't go to work. It's a lovely time for the family to play Sabbath Bible and nature games; to read good, true, character-building stories; to go walking in God's beautiful outdoors; and to visit the sick and lonely.

Yet who's to say the ancient Jews did not include most of these appropriate activities in their Sabbath keeping? Probably they did. So what went wrong?

The Missing Ingredient

Paul gave us a clue. He told Timothy, "The foundation of God standeth sure, having this seal, The Lord knoweth them that are his" (2 Timothy 2:19). So, the seal is placed on those whom God knows.

Jesus said much the same, with a very significant added comment: "I am the good shepherd, and know my sheep, and am known of mine" (John 10:14). Members of the Good Shepherd's flock are not only known by the Shepherd, they know the Shepherd. Know Him well enough to recognize His voice; know Him well enough to trust Him wherever He leads them. "My sheep hear my voice," Jesus said, "and I know them, and *they follow me*" (John 10:27, emphasis supplied). Apparently they believe what He says and keep His commandments.

Jesus said the Jews of His day did neither. "Ye believe not, because ye are not of my sheep," He told the Jews in the temple a few months before He died (verse 26). Rather than accept His testimony, they picked up stones to kill Him—proving He had told the truth.

They kept the Sabbath, but they never got acquainted with the Lord of the Sabbath. Even when Jesus lived among them, they were too busy, too proud, too locked up in their preconceptions to get to know Him. Jesus interrupted the triumphal entry to weep, "If only you had known!" (see Luke 19:42).

The mystery is removed. The seal of God is not some magical mark placed arbitrarily on one Christian and not on another. Nor even on one Sabbath keeper and not on another just as worthy. It is no more mysterious or arbitrary than a marriage certificate.

The officiating minister hands the certificate to the wedded couple after a period of time in which the young man and woman have developed a friendship so mutually satisfying that they know they will love and trust each other for the rest of their lives. The success of the marriage does not depend on the minister or on the certificate. It depends on the friendship, the love, and the trust that have developed between the couple before the wedding.

A Day to Fall in Love

Young American and Canadian couples date. A date is to marriage very much what Sabbath keeping is to the seal of God; the marriage certificate is the seal. Some dates are purely casual; on others, the man is eager and the woman indifferent, or the woman more eager than the man. But the dating that leads to successful, lifelong marriage is the dating in which both fall in love as they get to know each other better.

This kind of dating produces permanent, till-death-us-do-part marriages. The marriage certificate merely recognizes the loving, trusting friendship that has already developed; it makes the marriage official, that's all.

In Sabbath keeping, God is always an eager partner. However, He is wise enough to know when He isn't wanted. He never forces Himself on a Sabbath keeper who wishes He weren't around. But as in the kind of dating that leads to marriage, it is the Sabbath keeping that develops friendship, love, and trust between a Christian and his God that will be capped with God's seal. In a very real sense—and not unlike the way the engagement seals a marriage some time before the wedding—the Sabbath keeper may be sealed long before the "seal of God" is officially placed on his or her forehead.

Is Sabbath Keeping "Legalism"?

Some may ask, If falling in love with God is what counts, why make so much of Sabbath keeping, sundown worship, church attendance, etc.? Isn't it better to develop the friendship without involving all these legalistic requirements?

Apparently love for God cannot develop without the time that is involved in Sabbath keeping—much as human love will not develop without time together. Both partners had better be on time for the date. Just so, Sabbath keepers must keep their appointments with God promptly and communicate with Him while they are together.

Speaking of the troubles of the last days, Ellen White wrote, "Satan will, if possible, prevent them [the people of God] from obtaining a preparation to stand in that day. He will so arrange affairs as to hedge up their way, entangle them with earthly treasures, cause them to carry a heavy, wearisome burden, that their hearts may be overcharged with the cares of this life and the day of trial may come upon them as a thief" (*The Great Controversy*, pp. 625, 626). God provided the Sabbath to give us time to escape these entanglements and to come apart and develop an everlasting, loving friendship with Him.

Is Sabbath keeping "legalism"? As soon as a loving

friendship develops between a Christian and God, the Christian will want to keep the Sabbath. Jesus said, "If you love me, you will obey what I command" (John 14:15, NIV). On the other hand, if anyone says, "I love God," but he is not keeping the Sabbath, he may fit John's description of the man who is "a liar, and the truth is not in him" (1 John 2:4).

Besides, what eager lover would want to stop dating his beloved?

And what would we say of this young man? He assures us, "I'm going to marry Kathy," but when we ask, "How often do you date?" he says, "Oh, it's been a year, maybe two years since we dated." So we ask, "Then you stay home every evening?" He says, "No, no. I go to everything that's interesting. Sometimes I take Joan or Chris." "Well, then," we ask, "do you and Kathy write often?" to which he says, "I don't write her, but she writes me. She doesn't know I never read her letters. But I'm going to marry her. I'll show you our marriage certificate someday." What would you say to him? What would you say to someone who says, "I don't keep the Sabbath, but I'm sure I'll get God's seal"?

Holding Hands With Jesus

When this friendship with God has fully developed, we can claim one of the most beautiful promises God ever gave human beings. Jesus said, "My sheep hear my voice, and I know them, and they follow me: and I give unto them eternal life; and they shall never perish, *neither shall any man pluck them out of my hand.* My Father, which gave them me: is greater than all; and *no man is able to pluck them out of my Father's hand*" (John 10:27-29, emphasis supplied).

Whether we escape to the mountains or are locked away in some loathsome dungeon, we need not fear that under the pressure of the persecution we will lose our hold on God. In that dreadful time, it will not be our grip on God that will count for so much. It will be God's grip on us. God the Father will be standing on one side of us, holding that hand. God the Son will be on the other side, holding that hand. They will never let go, no matter what. They've promised. No one, certainly not the dragon, will be able to pull us out of Their hands.

That beautiful promise tells us again that God will be an impregnable refuge in the storm. Surely it is assurance enough for even the most timid Christian.

Chapter 5

God's Champions

(Revelation 14:1-5)

I looked, and, lo, a Lamb stood on the mount Sion, and with him an hundred and forty and four thousand. . . . These are they which follow the Lamb. . . . For they are without fault before the throne. Revelation 14:1-5.

There must be something very special about the 144,000. Jesus is so proud of them. He talked to John about them in the most complimentary terms in three separate visions.

He mentioned them first in the vision of the seven seals, in which He told John He planned to delay the final events specifically to give angels time to seal the 144,000 with the seal of the living God (see Revelation 7:1-8). He talks about them here, in the "great controversy vision," announcing His intention to gather them closely around Himself on the sea of glass before the throne, with the heavenly orchestra accompanying them and the angels hushed to hear them sing. Soon, in the vision of the plagues, we'll find Him congratulating them for conquering the beast, his image, mark, and name (see chapter 15:2).

Jesus seems so eager to draw attention to them that He even interrupts Himself. As proof, note that the first five verses of Revelation 14 belong chronologically at the end of the chapter. One might even say they should have been held over for the discussion of the millennium in chapter 20.

But apparently Jesus could not wait till then. He had just told John how cruelly the beast will persecute His valiant followers for refusing to honor the beast's image and mark, and He can wait no longer to tell how richly He plans to reward such outstanding loyalty. He will surround this faithful band with unprecedented splendor and unrivaled honor. So pleased is He with the way they have lived for Him on earth that He will associate Himself with them wherever He travels in heaven. He will even write His own name on their foreheads, marking them His special property, His "treasured possession," for all eternity.

What makes them so special? Others have obeyed God in difficult times. Many have suffered martyrdom. All have received His thanks and blessing. But none of them have won this effulgent outpouring of Divine gratitude. Why?

Study the 144,000 in the setting of the great controversy, and the mystery is solved.

God's Unanswerable Defense

From the beginning, Satan charged that God was unjust in requiring the angels to keep His law. He claimed they would be better off if they didn't. After Adam and Eve fell, Satan pointed to their failure as proof that created beings could not keep the law even in the pleasant surroundings of Eden.

To prove that His law was right and just and good and that even human beings could keep it, Jesus left heaven, came to earth as a man, and lived for thirty-three years in perfect conformity to God's will. Here, indeed, was evidence that Satan was wrong and God right; the loyal angels in heaven and devout Christians on earth accepted the evidence as convincing proof.

But some sinners whom God wanted to save raised questions. Was Jesus altogether and completely the same as man, conquering Satan the same way we must? Or did He have extra help? Devout Christians and loyal angels joined God in answering Yes to the first question and No to the second. But we can easily believe that God recognized the questions' validity. After all, Jesus was God before He became man; more than that, He was God while He was man—and that could be said of no created being. God wants the service of love based on evidence; yet here were questions that could be raised again and cause trouble far in the distant future.

God Needs Transformed Sinners

If only there were men and women degraded by thousands of years of sin—themselves practicing sinners, debauched by unlawful habits—who would so far yield themselves to God and cooperate with His Spirit that they would abandon their sinful ways and be transformed into the likeness of Christ. If only these sinners would so fully conform to His will that they could live in the presence of God—while still on earth—without an intercessor. If there could only be a few like that, God would have evidence to cite in defense of His claim that what He asked could be done, and that those who obeyed were better off for doing so.

Suppose a large group of men and women and boys and girls like this demonstrated that total conformity to God's law and obedient respect for His counsel produce the best of characters even in the worst of times.

Suppose, further, that this group lived at the very end of time, when the human race was its most degraded, when Satan and his demons had sharpened their vicious skills with 6,000 years of cruelty, when the image of God was almost totally stamped out of man's heart and the knowledge of God erased from his mind, when the earth was filled with violence worse than before the Flood, and every imagination was only evil continually—and suppose there were actually as many as 144,000 in this faultless band, all totally loyal even when God's mercy no longer pleaded for the race and Satan's malice was permitted unhindered expression. With such a band as that, God would have evidence in defense of His goodness and justice so overwhelming none could gainsay it, now or ever.

And that is what the 144,000 are all about. That's why God is so pleased with them. They are His champions. They provide Him with an unchallengeable defense. That's why He plans to honor them with glory, certify them with His signature, and take them with Him wherever He goes, to answer whatever questions may come up regarding the fairness of His government and the success of the plan of salvation.

If God is excited by the 144,000, we can be too. They demonstrate that we, each one of us, can be fully conformed to the will of God. We can be transformed, like them, into His likeness. There is no limit to the beauty of character that, with God's help, we can attain to. We can have total victory over the sin in our lives. We, too, can be "without fault before the throne."

Total Victory Possible

Some Christians say we don't really need to gain victory over sin, that God is too kind to destroy sinners. But that sounds so much like the lie Satan told Eve—"ye shall not surely die"—that it cannot possibly be true. Paul said, "The wages of sin is death" (Romans 6:23); and Ellen White wrote, "The love of God does not lead Him to excuse sin" (*Christ's Object Lessons*, p. 316).

Again, many Christians say that sinners cannot keep God's law. But Paul wrote, "I can do all things through Christ which strengtheneth me" (Philippians 4:13). Ellen White wrote, "Satan had claimed that it was impossible for man to obey God's commandments; and in our own strength it is true that we cannot obey them. But Christ came in the form of humanity, and by His perfect obedience He proved that humanity and divinity combined can obey every one of God's precepts. . . . When a soul receives Christ, he receives power to live the life of Christ" (*ibid.*, p. 314). In another place she said, "As the will of man co-operates with the will of God, it becomes omnipotent" (*ibid.*, p. 333). That should be power enough, surely!

Occasionally we hear that sinners can make some progress toward sanctification, but that, nowadays, human flesh is too weak or too degraded to obey all God's law; for total sanctification we must wait until God makes miraculous changes in our character at the moment of translation. Let's look at this closely.

Saved "to the Uttermost" Now

We Adventists insist that new converts must give up drinking and smoking, they must keep the Sabbath holy, and they must so far overcome selfishness as to pay a full tithe on their earnings. If new converts object that we make hard demands, we pat them on the back and assure them we'll pray for them; "God will give you victory, Brother." And God does give victory; we've all seen it happen. But is there a limit to the victories God can provide? Are there some sinful practices Jesus can remove, even from besotted drunkards and the grossly immoral, while at the same time there are other bad habits He cannot eliminate? If this were true, wouldn't Satan have won the great controversy? He claimed from the first that he was stronger than Jesus. Can it be true that once Satan controls a sinner's life Jesus is too weak to unseat him; Jesus can make a few inroads around the edges, as it were, but He can't take full possession? Perish the thought! Jesus saves "to the uttermost" (Hebrews 7:25).

Moreover, the 144,000 are able to stand in the presence of God without an intercessor while they "are living upon the earth" (*The Great Controversy*, p. 425). They are cleansed from every spot and wrinkle *before* Jesus comes.

Some Christians say they are leaving the salvation of their souls entirely to Christ. This, they say, is the true meaning of salvation by faith. To struggle with their bad habits would be, by their definition, salvation by works. If they are caught yielding to a besetting sin, they excuse themselves with the defense that God has not seen fit to remove this temptation from them yet.

By Faith and Diligent Effort

Ellen White wrote, "There are many who profess Christ, but who never become mature Christians. They admit that man is fallen, that his faculties are weakened, that he is unfitted for moral achievement, but they say that Christ has borne all the burden, all the suffering, all the self-denial, and they are willing to let Him bear it. They say that there is nothing for them to do but to believe; but Christ said, 'If any man will come after me, let him deny himself, and take up his cross, and follow me' (Matt. 16:24)" (*Maranatha*, p. 236).

"There is earnest warfare before all who would subdue the evil tendencies that strive for the mastery" (*The Great Controversy*, p. 490).

"Those who are living upon the earth when the intercession of Christ shall cease in the sanctuary above are to stand in the sight of a holy God without a mediator. [She's talking about those who want to belong to the 144,000.] Their robes must be spotless, their characters must be purified from sin by the blood of sprinkling. *Through the grace of God and their own diligent effort* they must be conquerors in the battle with evil. While the investigative judgment is going forward in heaven, while the sins of penitent believers are being removed from the sanctuary, there is to be a special work of purification, of putting away of sin, among God's people upon earth" (*ibid.*, p. 425, emphasis supplied).

"Our precious Saviour invites us to join ourselves to Him, to unite our weakness to His strength, our ignorance to His wisdom, our unworthiness to His merits. . . . It rests with us to co-operate with the agencies which Heaven employs in the work of conforming our characters to the divine model" (*ibid.*, p. 623).

And what will be the result of this joint effort? The 144,000 are "without fault," and we can be too. Listen.

More Than Conquerors

Jesus "is ready to purify your heart, and give you the sanctification of His Spirit. As you commit yourself to His service, He will be at your right hand to help you. Day by day you will be strengthened and ennobled. Looking to the Saviour for help, you will be a conqueror, yes, more than a conqueror, over the temptations that beset you. You will become more and more like Christ" (*Counsels to Teachers*, p. 490).

"A holy temper, a Christlike life, is accessible to every repenting, believing child of God" (*The Desire of Ages*, p. 311).

"By His perfect obedience He has made it possible for every human being to obey God's commandments. When we submit ourselves to Christ, the heart is united with His heart, the will is merged in His will, the mind becomes one with His mind, the thoughts are brought into captivity to Him; we live His life" (*Christ's Object Lessons*, p. 312).

"You need never yield to temptation; for One stands by your side who is able to keep you from falling" (*Maranatha*, p. 225).

Fully Reflecting Christ's Character

"Christ is waiting with longing desire for the manifestation of Himself in His church. When the character of Christ shall be perfectly reproduced in His people, then He will come to claim them as His own" (*Christ's Object Lessons*, p. 69). We know He will come. Then we can know just as certainly that His character will be perfectly reproduced in His people *before* He comes.

"Jesus will bring them [His people] forth as gold tried in the fire. Their earthliness will be removed, that through them the image of Christ may be perfectly revealed" (*Prophets and Kings*, p. 589).

"If you give yourself to Him, and accept Him as your Saviour, then . . . Christ changes the heart. . . . He will work in you to will and to do according to His good pleasure. . . . You will manifest the same spirit and do the same good works—works of righteousness, obedience" (*Steps to Christ*, pp. 62, 63).

"God has encircled the whole world with an atmosphere of grace. . . . All who choose to breathe this life-giving atmosphere will live and grow up to the stature of men and women in Christ Jesus. . . . Abiding in Him, you may flourish" (*ibid.*, pp. 68, 69).

Transformed Into His Likeness

"By loving Him, copying Him, depending wholly upon Him, . . . you are to be transformed into His likeness" (*ibid.*, p. 71).

"Not even by a thought could our Saviour be brought to yield to the power of temptation. . . . He had kept His Father's commandments, and there was no sin in Him that Satan could use to his advantage. This is the condition in which those must be found who shall stand in the time of trouble" (*The Great Controversy*, p. 623).

"If we consent, He [Christ] will so identify Himself with our thoughts and aims, so blend our hearts and minds into conformity to His will, that when obeying Him we shall be but carrying out our own impulses. The will, refined and sanctified, will find its highest delight in doing His service. When we know God as it is our privilege to know Him, our life will be a life of continual obedience. Through an appreciation of the character of Christ, through communion with God, sin will become hateful to us" (*The Desire of Ages*, p. 668).

"Christ is sitting for His portrait in every disciple. . . . All who consecrate soul, body, and spirit to God will be constantly receiving a new endowment of physical and mental power. The inexhaustible supplies of heaven are at their command. Christ gives them the breath of His own spirit, the life of His own life. The Holy Spirit puts forth its highest energies to work in heart and mind. The grace of God enlarges and multiplies their faculties, and every perfection of the divine nature comes to their assistance in the work of saving souls. Through co-operation with Christ they are complete in Him, and in their human weakness they are enabled to do the deeds of Omnipotence" (*ibid.*, p. 827).

Imagine being truly Christlike! As kind as Jesus. As generous as He was. As true and honest and pure and thoughtful and helpful and loving and caring. The list of beautiful attributes is as long as infinity, as all-embracing as the lovely character of God. The 144,000 will have them. All of them. We can have them, too, for we can be among that special group. Ellen White wrote, "Let us strive with all the power that God has given us to be among the hundred and forty-four thousand" (*Maranatha*, p. 241).

We don't have to be cross and grumpy anymore. Impure thoughts can be replaced with snow-white purity and perfect fidelity. Envy and jealousy can be gone forever, their places filled with generosity and genuine pleasure at others' success. We can be the kind of persons we (and our spouses and children) wish we were. The 144,000 prove it.

Lately some have raised questions about the nature of Christ. Did He come to the world with the nature of man after 4,000 years of sin, or with the nature of Adam before the Fall? Whichever it was, He won the victory over Satan for us, and now listen to what He wants to do for us. "Everyone who by faith obeys God's commandments, will reach the condition of sinlessness in which Adam lived before his transgression" (*Maranatha*, p. 224).

No Mediator, but Many Defenders

It sounds frightening to stand in the presence of God without a mediator, as if the redeemed must endure the final storm alone. But that's not what God says. The 144,000 don't have a mediator because they don't need one; they are faultless. But they need protection against Satan's cruel onslaughts, and God will provide them a multitude of defenders. Jesus will be very close.

"Angels will come to them in lonely cells, bringing light and peace from heaven. The prison will be as a palace" (*The Great Controversy*, p. 627).

"That God who cared for Elijah will not pass by one of His self-sacrificing children. He who numbers the hairs of their heads will care for them" (*ibid.*, p. 629).

"To human sight it will appear that the people of God must soon seal their testimony with their blood. . . . Could men see with heavenly vision, they would behold companies of angels that excel in strength stationed about those who have kept the word of Christ's patience. . . . They are waiting the word of their Commander to snatch them from their peril" (*ibid.*, p. 630).

"The heavenly sentinels, faithful to their trust, continue their watch. . . . None can pass the mighty guardians stationed about every faithful soul" (*ibid.*, p. 631).

Never doubt for a moment! God will certainly provide this special group a sure and certain refuge in the storm.

Chapter 6

Master Plot to Belittle Christ

(Revelation 14:6, 7)

I saw another angel fly in the midst of heaven, having the everlasting gospel to preach . . . , saying with a loud voice, Fear God . . . ; for the hour of his judgment is come: and worship him that made heaven, and earth. Revelation 14:6, 7.

To TV watchers, quick scene changes are commonplace. But in slow-moving A.D. 95, what did John think when the picture of the dragon lunging for the woman's Child suddenly gave place to scenes of a war in heaven . . . to views of a multi-horned beast coming out of the sea . . . to a clip of 144,000 saints singing on the sea of glass, and then to a flying angel shouting in midair? Was he a bit bewildered by all the fast changes? Or did he take them in stride? We must be sure to get to heaven to ask him.

Did he understand why an angel suddenly appeared in the middle of the "great controversy vision," right after the 144,000 fault-free saints sang their incomprehensible song? Did he, for a moment, wonder why an angel still preached to people on earth after the righteous had been transported to Paradise?

No doubt, when he thought about it later, he understood, as we do, that the three angels of Revelation 14 would proclaim their messages while the leopardlike beast with the horns and crowns recovered from his deadly wound and the two-horned, lamblike beast rose out of the earth and became a persecuting power. To put it simply, much of chapters 13 and 14 were fulfilled contemporaneously. Also, the three angels' messages were inserted here to help explain how the 144,000 developed their fault-free characters.

The Everlasting Gospel

The first angel preached the everlasting gospel. "Everlasting" affirms that the good news about salvation has always been the same. This corrects the false notion that New Testament salvation—in which sinners are saved by faith in Jesus—is new and better than Old Testament salvation, in which sinners are supposed to have been saved by offering innumerable animal sacrifices.

The fact is that God has saved sinners one way—and only one way—since Adam and Eve left Eden, that is, by faith in Jesus. This can be proved, surprisingly enough, by a bit of very simple arithmetic. The Bible tells us that there were as many as 600,000 Israelite men of military age (see Numbers 11:21). Adding the women, it is conservative to say there were more than a million people of responsible age in the total population. If each of these Israelites offered a sacrifice every time he or she sinned (say, once a day), the priests would have had to sacrifice at least one million animals every day. With a courtyard measuring only 150 feet long and 75 feet wide in which to prepare the animals (see Exodus 27:9-13), and only one altar measuring less than eight feet square to offer them on (Exodus 27:1), this was totally impossible. And where would sinners have found 365,000,000 sheep and oxen every year?

At Josiah's Passover (see 2 Chronicles 35), 41,400 animals swamped the priests. Even though most of the animals were roasted, then eaten by the worshipers rather than burned on the altar, the priests had to call on the Levites for help. The biblical historian notes that this was the largest Passover ever observed prior to the Babylonian Exile. The usual number of sacrificed animals must have been far fewer.

The evidence suggests that individual Israelites rarely offered an animal sacrifice. Probably some, even among the devout, never offered one. Many lived too far from Jerusalem to make the trip. For long periods at a time, the temple services were suspended due to national apostasy. In good times, the Passover lamb was eaten nationwide as a special meal, once a year, like Christmas and Thanksgiving dinners today; but we can safely assume that asking a priest to offer an animal on the altar was definitely not done every time an Israelite sinned.

What actually happened was that Moses directed the priests to offer a lamb every morning and evening, "two lambs of the first year day by day continually" (Exodus 29:38, 39). This continual burned offering served for all the people. It reminded them that Jesus would come and die for them and pointed their faith to Him as their Redeemer—just as the Bible today directs our faith to Jesus, who died to become our Saviour.

The gospel was the same then as now.

Unfortunately, many Israelites began to look only at the sacrificed animals and reasoned that they could sin freely provided they offered enough lambs, bullocks, and goats (see Micah 6:7, 8). Jesus corrected this erroneous idea, and the early church again preached the everlasting gospel. But by the Middle Ages, the gospel had been corrupted even worse than before, with penances and indulgences and other "works," so that millions believed their departed loved ones, no matter how badly they had sinned, gained instant entrance to heaven when their coins struck the bottom of an offering box. The Reformation corrected these false ideas, and we can say that, generally speaking, at the beginning of the nineteenth century—when the first angel began to fly—many Protestant ministers in the New World were preaching the everlasting gospel once more.

The Judgment Hour

If this were so, why did God ask them to preach anything more? The poet answers well: "They must upward still and onward who would keep abreast of truth."

Here God was faced with a familiar problem! On the way to

the cross, Jesus still had many things to tell the disciples which would have prepared their faith for the ordeal ahead; but because they weren't ready, He couldn't tell them (see John 16:12). As a result, when Jesus was arrested, the disciples deserted Him.

In the early 1800s, Christians needed to know that the judgment hour was near. Jesus was about to enter the second apartment of the heavenly sanctuary to examine the record of every professed Christian. Soon all who proved faithful would be sealed for eternity, their sins forever removed, replaced by the lovely character of Jesus. Those judged to have been unfaithful would be lost without recourse.

Ellen White explained just how important this knowledge is. She wrote, "The subject of the sanctuary and the investigative judgment should be clearly understood by the people of God. All need a knowledge for themselves of the position and work of their great High Priest. Otherwise it will be impossible for them to exercise the faith which is essential at this time or to occupy the position which God designs them to fill. . . .

"The sanctuary in heaven is the very center of Christ's work in behalf of men. It concerns every soul living upon the earth. It opens to view the plan of redemption, bringing us down to the very close of time and revealing the triumphant issue of the contest between righteousness and sin" (*The Great Controversy*, p. 488).

Unfortunately, most Christians who were teaching the everlasting gospel in the early 1800s rejected the judgment-hour message. This set the stage for them to reject the next important truth God wanted them to preach, the vital significance of the seventh-day Sabbath.

Worship the Creator!

In addition to preaching the everlasting gospel and announcing the judgment, the first angel reminded the world to worship God as Creator. This drew attention to the Sabbath as the memorial of creation. Adventists have historically stressed this aspect of creation, and rightly so, considering the important part faithful Sabbath keeping will play in the final events.

But there is much more to the first angel's message than Sabbath keeping, vital as that is. For one thing, note the time when this call to worship the Creator came. It follows right after the judgment-hour message. The judgment began in 1844. The theory of evolution launched its public assault on creation with the publication of Charles Darwin's *Origin of Species* in 1859, fifteen years after 1844. The sequence of the two events, as mentioned in the prophecy, matches the sequence in which they took place in history. Evidently God knows future events as well as He claims to. We look on the commencement of the investigative judgment as a sign of the nearness of Christ's advent; we may also see the modern teaching of evolution as additional confirmation that the second coming is near.

The evolution/creation debate is not merely an argument between scientists and theologians. Evolution is part of a sophisticated plot by Satan to accomplish what he set out to do at the beginning of the great controversy, to belittle Christ. He has succeeded so well among many Christians that we Adventists must beware not to let ourselves get caught in the science/theology trap. We can be proud that the first Christian to mount a successful scientific attack on evolution was a Seventh-day Adventist, George McCready Price. We should be grateful for several others who have systematically gathered evidence showing that the evolution theory is not scientifically impregnable, but riddled with unscientific weaknesses. At the same time, we should not expect scientific arguments alone to swing the scientific world to our side.

You see, never before has so much scientific evidence in favor of creation flooded the world. Through the very scientists who deny Him, God has chosen to reveal the marvels of His created works, from the most remote distances of outer space to the minute inner recesses of the smallest atoms. Every new scientific discovery opens the door to more. Knowledge of what God has done doubles every two or three years, so that anyone who denies the Creator today is without excuse. Even so, university graduates, steeped in so much science that they laugh at Dark Ages peasants who believed that their clanking coins conducted suffering souls to eternal bliss, still embrace the most naive notions about their own origins. How can we expect to change their views if our approach is limited only to science?

Evolution Is a Religion

The theory of evolution is a religion that Satan wants the world to accept in place of Christianity. We say this because evolution seeks to answer the same basic questions Christianity answers; and the answers are strangely similar, though poles apart. Look at it this way:

1. Christianity attempts to answer two basic questions: Why do people die? What must we do to live forever? Christianity answers these questions by saying that people die because they sin; to live they must become righteous.

2. Christianity defines righteousness by the Ten Commandments and the life of Jesus Christ.

3. Christianity demands a sacrifice. Jesus Christ chose Himself, the one fully righteous Person, to be this sacrifice.

4. And Christianity promises that all who sin—that is, all of us—by placing our faith in the divine Sacrifice, may become righteous and live forever.

Compare this with the theory of evolution.

1. Evolution seeks to answer the same two basic questions: Why do people die? and, What must they do to live forever?

2. Evolution answers by talking about "the survival of the fittest." Fitness is needed for survival. Lack of fitness results in death. Note the similarity here. "Fitness" in evolution corresponds to "righteousness" in Christianity.

3. Evolution also demands a sacrifice—but what a different sacrifice! In evolution, "natural selection" chooses the victims. All the unfit die, all the millions upon millions of us.

4. And what does all this death produce? Only this: a vague, undefined promise that out of this vast mass of moldering mortals one truly fit person—the "fittest"—will survive to live, though no one knows when or where.

Note that no evolutionary scientist has ever defined ultimate fitness, so no one can be sure whether evolution has been advancing toward it, or not. And there is no way to tell. So there is no certainty that this lucky "fittest" person will ever evolve. All that is known for sure is that everyone else—everyone now living—will die . . . and rot.

I find it fascinating that in Christianity the one and only righteous Person died so that all the unrighteous may live if they choose; whereas in evolution, in the vague hope that one fit person may eventually survive, all the unfit must die, and we have no choice in the matter at all.

Who would want to choose this totally hopeless religion and reject Christianity?

There is no place for Jesus in evolution. Jesus wasn't around when life began. His death on Calvary was a pious irrelevancy, because belief in the blood atonement is not the route to fitness. And His second coming in power and glory is a puerile fantasy; since there is no resurrection, Jesus no longer exists; and because there is no heaven, there is no "Father's house" to take His people to. How evolution does belittle Christ!

Some Christians, trying to hold onto their religion and still appear scientifically acceptable, have interpreted the seven days of creation week as seven long periods of time. But this, too, puts Jesus where Satan wants Him. Too weak to do the job so fast, Jesus nevertheless claims that He did and then commands us to do all our work in six days and worship Him on the seventh—which makes Him a liar and a tyrant.

We can be confident that Jesus told the truth on Mount Sinai when we remember that He was surrounded by angels and observed by all the heavenly host. Jesus could have deceived the Israelites, but not the angels; for they were present at creation and would have caught a lie at once. Jesus would have lost the great controversy right then. The fact that the angels and the heavenly host approved Jesus' claim is all the proof we need.

Children of a Lesser God

Perhaps the greatest tragedy of the modern theory of evolution is what it has done to damage the faith of a generation—

faith in God and faith in itself. Too many of today's young people, along with many of their parents, don't know who they are or what they are supposed to do with their lives. To them there is no god, and if there is, he is a weak, ineffective thing who brought the world into existence through a long series of trial and error. He is totally out of touch with today's youth and offers nothing for their future.

Not so for youth brought up to believe in divine creation. They know they are the children of the living God, Creator of heaven and earth, the great God who holds the universe in His hands. He commands the stars, and they do His bidding. The vast organization of heavenly angels stands ready to come or go at His request. For One so wise and powerful, the creating of our world was but a week's quick work. He merely spoke, and everything came into existence just as He wanted it.

These children know, too, that this great, all-powerful, all-wise God loves them. He cares for each of them as if not another soul on earth required His attention. He has a place for each in His service. And His plans for them include not just time alone, but eternity as well.

How long will our nation's youth be taught that they are the unwanted children of some lesser god, instead of the beloved children of the greatest God that ever was or ever will be? One who is well able to provide them a refuge in the last great, terrible storm?

Thank God the angel told us to worship Jesus as our Creator!

Chapter 7

Beware Lest We Fall!

(Revelation 14:8)

There followed another angel, saying, Babylon is fallen, is fallen. Revelation 14:8.

"I was born in a little village in Scotland in 1824. I had four brothers and six sisters, but our house had only two rooms. The room at one end was my mother's domain. It was our dining room and kitchen and parlor and bedroom, all in one. The room at the other end was my father's workshop, where he made stockings to sell to the storekeepers at Dumfries.

"Between these rooms was a very small room we called the closet. It had only enough space for a bed, a little table, and a chair. This was the sanctuary of our home. Many times a day we saw our father go in there and shut the door. We children got to understand by a sort of spiritual instinct (for the thing was too sacred to be talked about) that he was praying there for us. Occasionally we heard his voice pleading as if for life, and we learned to slip in and out past that door on tiptoe so as not to disturb his conversation with the Lord. We knew why our father's face always shone with a happy light. It was a reflection from the Divine Presence."

Thus begins the autobiography of James G. Paton, Presbyterian missionary to the Pacific Islands when cannibals still ate the dead who died in battle, then strangled their widows and ate them too.

It is appropriate to insert this bit of church history into our study of Revelation, because of the way Adventists interpret the second angel's message. Back in 1843 and 1844, when

Protestant churches began to disfellowship their members who believed in the nearness of the advent, Millerites began to preach that they were not only Babylon, but they were Babylon fallen. Adventists still teach much the same. Perhaps there is comfort—if not pride—in calling *them* Babylon and *ourselves* the remnant. But those churches were so much like us, especially in their beginnings, that a closer look may serve as both challenge and warning. In many ways they were ahead of us.

Their Dedicated Missionaries

Adventists sent our first missionary overseas in 1874. It was more than eighty years earlier, in 1793, when the Baptists of Britain sponsored William Carey to India, where he translated all or parts of the Bible into some forty different languages. The American Congregationalists sent Adoniram Judson to Burma in 1812. Home from Africa on a brief furlough, Robert Moffat spoke wherever possible about the African people and their need for the Saviour. His oft-repeated comment, "In the light of the morning sun, I have seen the smoke of a thousand villages where no missionary has ever been," inspired David Livingstone to follow in his footsteps and to go far beyond them. Livingstone left for the mission field in 1840, age twenty-seven, sponsored by the London Missionary Society.

The list could go on and on. Thousands of dedicated Christian young people gave their lives to mission service before the first Adventist foreign missionary set sail. And theirs were not year-long assignments; they were life commitments. These earnest young missionaries buried their little babies and their spouses in lonely graves; and when invited to return home, they answered that they could not, for part of themselves now permanently belonged to the mission field.

Their Well-attended Camp Meetings

Adventists held their first camp meeting, officially sponsored by the General Conference and announced in the *Review and Herald*, in Michigan in 1868. About 2,000 attended, both Adventists and non-Adventists. Many were converted, and there was a general feeling that the Lord had blessed the gathering. It was decided to have more camp meetings the following year.

The Protestant churches in North America had their first camp meeting nearly seventy years earlier, in Logan County, Kentucky, in 1801. Estimates of the attendance range from 12,000 to 25,000.

It was essentially a spontaneous gathering. Some Presbyterian ministers appointed a communion service and invited scattered believers to attend. Kentucky was very much on the frontier in those days; most Kentucky settlers in 1801—like most Adventists in 1868—lived too far from a church to attend regularly. Peter Cartwright, who served as a Methodist circuit rider for fifty years, was a teenager at the time. He lived nearby and probably attended the camp meeting for a while. He wrote later, "Seemingly unexpected by ministers or people, the mighty power of God was displayed in a very extraordinary manner; many were moved to tears, and bitter and loud crying for mercy. The meeting was protracted for weeks. Ministers of almost all denominations flocked in from far and near. The meeting was kept up by night and day. Thousands heard of the mighty work, and came on foot, on horseback, in carriages and wagons. It was supposed that there were in attendance at times during the meeting from twelve to twenty-five thousand people. . . .

"Stands were erected in the woods from which preachers of different churches proclaimed repentance toward God and faith in our Lord Jesus Christ. It was not unusual for one, two, three, and four to seven preachers to be addressing the listening thousands at the same time from the different stands erected for the purpose. And it was supposed, by eye and ear witnesses, that between one and two thousand people were converted to God during the meeting."

The Protestant denominations, especially the Presbyterian, Methodist, and Baptist, held many camp meetings after that. None were as large as the first, simply because there were so many of them. It was quite common to have preachers from different denominations present, preaching in different areas of a campground, each surrounded by a group of eager listeners. The people could choose the best to listen to, which must have stimulated those preachers to prepare their sermons well. The settlers brought their Bibles and went home to conduct daily worship in their families. Observers expressed amazement at the improvement of morals in surrounding communities following a camp meeting. The presence of the Holy Spirit was convincingly demonstrated by the large number of conversions. Baptist membership grew to nearly two million by the outbreak of the War Between the States in 1861. Methodists, numbering only 5,000 at the turn of the century, grew in the same six decades to be almost as numerous as the Baptists.

Colleges to Train Their Ministers

Adventists have a dozen colleges in North America besides many more around the world. We know that the primary reason for establishing them was to prepare ministers and other workers for the church. In the United States, from the days of the first Puritans until the Civil War, 182 permanent colleges were founded. Almost without exception, all were established to provide ministers for the various denominations.*

Even the granddaddy of all American colleges, Harvard, was founded to provide a trained ministry. In 1636, while Cambridge was still a struggling frontier village of a couple dozen houses surrounded by a wooden fence, the Puritan ministers (Congregationalists) called for the establishing of a college, because, they said, they dreaded "to leave an illiterate ministry to the churches when our present ministers shall lie in the Dust." A later president reported how well Harvard fulfilled this original design; during the years 1636 to 1692, he said, the college was "conducted as a theological institution."

*If you wonder why these colleges are counted "until the Civil War," it is because the figures and most of the quotations in this section are taken from *The Founding of American Colleges and Universities Before the Civil War* by Donald G. Tewksbury.

The Episcopalians in 1693 founded William and Mary College at Williamsburg to provide pastors for their congregations in Virginia.

When Congregationalists and Presbyterians decided to walk different paths, the Presbyterians founded Yale (1701) "for the upholding and propagating of the Christian protestant Religion by a succession of Learned and Orthodox men."

Except that there were no Adventists in 1833 when Wabash College was founded, this next statement could have appeared in the *Adventist Review* in connection with the founding of an Adventist college: "We then proceeded in a body to the intended location in the primeval forest, and there kneeling in the snow we dedicated the grounds to the Father, the Son, and the Holy Ghost, for a Christian College."

After founding Brown University in Rhode Island in 1765, the Baptists waited till 1820 to found Colby College in Maine. In the next four decades they established twenty-three more, including George Washington University in the District of Columbia, Baylor in Texas, and Colgate and Vassar in New York; all—except Vassar!—to prepare young men for the Baptist ministry. The twenty-five institutions were widely scattered, located in nineteen of the thirty-four states.

The Methodists were at first skeptical of the highly educated ministry. By 1830 they saw that this attitude must change and established Randolph-Macon College in Virginia. In the next thirty years they founded thirty-three more colleges, including Emory in Georgia, DePauw in Indiana, Northwestern in Illinois, Duke in North Carolina. Like the Baptists, they scattered their colleges over the country to be close to their members—which helps explain why Adventists located our colleges all over North America too.

There isn't space to examine many others, but some readers may find it interesting to note that when the Congregational and Presbyterian churches worked together in 1855 to establish the University of California, it was to provide ministers for the West.

Their Many Benevolent Societies

The first sixty years of the nineteenth century might be called the age of the benevolent societies. For every human vice, the Protestant churches of North America had a society to combat it. For every virtue, a Protestant society existed to promote it.

During this time the Bible societies were organized. Sunday Schools trace their origin to this period. Mission societies sprang up in most Protestant denominations, both foreign mission societies to convert the heathen to Christ, and home mission societies to claim the western frontier for the Lord. There were abolition societies to free the slaves and temperance societies to combat drunkenness and close saloons. And the Northeast became known as the "burned-over district" from the frequency and intensity of the evangelistic campaigns that sought to win sinners to the Saviour.

Their Lessons for Us

These Protestant churches, in the sincerity of their faith and the zeal of their mission, sound so much like the Adventist Church in its early days, it's almost frightening. If they could be all of that, and fall, what's to prevent us from falling too?

Paul wrote the Corinthians, "Let him that thinketh he standeth take heed lest he fall" (1 Corinthians 10:12).

The Protestant churches were a powerful force for good in the United States prior to the Civil War. They never regained that position afterward. How much was this weakness due to their failure to receive the additional light God offered them in the first angel's message?

As Protestantism declined, Catholicism and spiritism and agnosticism grew stronger, healing the deadly wound. Prophecy does not indicate that the Adventist Church will cease to be the remnant church; but it includes a serious message about lukewarmness and a solemn warning about being spat from the Saviour's mouth. Maybe this is a good time to review them.

Their Contribution to Us

Adventists point to our interpretation of the heavenly sanctuary as a unique contribution we have made to Christian theology, and that observation is valid. But let us not forget how much we have received from other churches, the ones we so often call Babylon.

Our Bibles, whatever versions we use, all came from non-Adventists.

Most of the hymns we sing were composed by non-Adventists.

The basic Protestant belief, that we are justified by faith in Christ, came to us from the Lutherans.

The comforting assurance that our eternal destiny is not decided by some human priest who claims to have the keys of the kingdom, but by God, who knows the end from the beginning, came to us from John Calvin, founder of the Congregational and Presbyterian churches.

The stimulating certainty that God lets us choose whether we will be saved, then works with us to sanctify our lives to a fitness for heaven came to us from the Methodists.

The sensible practice of baptizing only persons old enough to understand the meaning of baptism came to us from the Baptists.

The restful knowledge that the dead do not writhe in hell but sleep till the resurrection came from members of several churches, none of them Adventist.

The Sabbath was brought to our attention by a Seventh Day Baptist.

The nearness of the second coming was preached first by a Baptist.

The true meaning of cleansing the sanctuary was channeled from heaven through an erstwhile Methodist.

The earliest guidance on health reform came from a member of the Christian Connection.

How much we owe these other denominations and their members! Let us thank them and pray for them that they too may be saved. For without them and the knowledge about Jesus that they handed us, we would have no hope.

Good News About Them

Ellen White wrote some good news about them. In spite of the way the Millerites interpreted the second angel's message in 1844, she said, "The message of the second angel did not reach its complete fulfillment in 1844. The churches then experienced a moral fall, in consequence of their refusal of the light of the advent message; but *that fall was not complete*. . . . Notwithstanding the spiritual darkness and alienation from God that exist in the churches which constitute Babylon, *the great body of Christ's true followers are still to be found in their communion*" (*The Great Controversy*, pp. 389, 390, emphasis supplied).

So our prayers can still be answered. The missionary literature we send out, the kindness and skill of our doctors and nurses, the messages beamed over radio and television will yet result in leading men and women and children in other churches, both Protestant and Catholic, to the additional truth of the three angels' messages. We have little time left, but there still is some. Let's use it for all it's worth.

Then they too will find God a benevolent refuge in the gathering storm.

Chapter 8

A Refuge From the Storm

(Revelation 14:9-12)

Here is the patience of the saints: here are they that keep the commandments of God, and the faith of Jesus. Revelation 14:12.

All who remember the agony that gripped America when John F. Kennedy died will sympathize with the deep concern of young Isaiah when good King Uzziah passed away. So many problems beset Judah! Israel and Syria were constant threats to the small nation. Would they seize this moment of weakness to invade and destroy? Would the new king measure up to the many challenges? Jerusalem was full of rumors, and the wisest men were perplexed.

But in that year of confusion and turmoil, the prophet's attention was drawn to a scene of surpassing peace and tranquility. He says, "In the year that king Uzziah died I saw also the Lord sitting upon a throne, high and lifted up" (Isaiah 6:1).

For a few glorious moments, angels drew back the veil between earth and heaven. At once Isaiah's outlook changed. The events of earth which had seemed so overwhelming assumed their true proportions. Human dynasties suddenly seemed feeble and transient beside the eternal majesty of the Most High. The strife of men, which had worried him so much, became foolish and petty in the presence of the calm serenity, the unbroken peace, of the everlasting God.

That personal revelation of God's transcendent majesty steadied and strengthened Isaiah through the rest of his life. When highly exalted under King Hezekiah, he remained humble as in the presence of a greater King. When persecuted to the death by the wicked Manasseh, he fixed his faith in Him who is above all earthly trial, finally hiding his life willingly in the life of Him who is eternal.

All who live till Jesus comes will need the same unswerving, confident faith Isaiah had.

For, make no mistake about it, a time of trouble is coming for God's people greater than anything Isaiah faced. Anyone who, at that time, gives up his allegiance to God for the sake of buying and selling a few earthly commodities, will cut himself off forever from eating freely of the tree of life. To avoid the wrath of the dragon will be to incur the displeasure of God. To protract one's earthly life a little while will be at the price of life everlasting.

God revealed to John, in the "great controversy vision," the final end of all who worship the beast and his image and receive his mark in forehead or hand. John heard the third angel announce that they will be "tormented with fire and brimstone in the presence of the holy angels, and in the presence of the Lamb: and the smoke of their torment ascendeth up for ever and ever: and they have no rest day nor night" (Revelation 14:10, 11).

Here is the most fearsome passage in all Scripture. One cries out, "How can I avoid such terrible punishment? When the wine of God's wrath is poured into the cup of His indignation, what must I do to be safe?"

Patience, Obedience, Faith

Happily for us, God gave John the answer. "Here," He said, "is the patience of the saints: here are they that keep the commandments of God, and the faith of Jesus" (verse 12).

The faithful saints need *patience*, because the final trial will probably last longer and certainly be more severe than they anticipate.

They *keep the commandments of God.* The habit of obedience, developed in peaceful times, holds them faithful in adversity.

And they have *the faith of Jesus*. This, in the final analysis, is what does most to keep them loyal. It helps them say with Paul, "I know whom I have believed, and am persuaded that he is able to keep that which I have committed unto him" (2 Timothy 1:12).

This is the faith that sustained Jesus on the cross, when "hope did not present to Him His coming forth from the grave a conqueror, or tell Him of the Father's acceptance of the sacrifice. He feared that sin was so offensive to God that Their separation was to be eternal." In that awful hour, when our destiny trembled in the balance, in what did Jesus place His trust? "He . . . relied upon the evidence of His Father's acceptance heretofore given Him. He was acquainted with the character of His Father; He understood His justice, His mercy, and His great love. By faith He rested in Him whom it had ever been His joy to obey. . . . By faith, Christ was victor" (*The Desire of Ages*, pp. 753, 756).

"God is our refuge and strength," sang the psalmist. Moses wrote, "The eternal God is thy refuge, and underneath are the everlasting arms" (Psalm 46:1; Deuteronomy 33:27). Jesus' faith was an intelligent, unswerving confidence in Him who is, for all who know Him, a "covert from the tempest," the one safe refuge from the storm that is about to break in fury on the world (see Isaiah 32:2).

How to Have This Faith

To have the faith of Jesus, we must know God. Isaiah saw Him, and his faith was established. Moses pleaded, "I beseech thee, shew me thy glory," and "the Lord passed by before him, and proclaimed, The Lord, The Lord God, merciful and gracious, longsuffering, and abundant in goodness and truth, keeping mercy for thousands, forgiving iniquity and transgression and sin, and that will by no means clear the guilty" (Exodus 33:18; 34:6, 7).

Ask God to reveal Himself to you. He will. Do not expect visions or dreams; God is very economical with visions, and dreams are too easily faked. Jesus' faith was based on evidence, knowledge, and understanding. He "relied upon the evidence" His Father had given Him; He "was acquainted with" God's character; He "understood" God's justice, mercy, and love. Ask God to help you see evidences of His love and to understand and appreciate what you see, and your request will be answered. Not all at once perhaps, but gradually your faith in Him will grow and flourish till you, too, have the faith of Jesus.

Faith From Nature

Gaze up on a clear, moonless night and watch the stars gliding silently across the sky. Stay till a fierce wind drives in a dark layer of storm clouds. Lightning strikes around you; thunder crashes overhead. The stars are completely hidden. But wait on a while longer, till the thunder rumbles far off in the distance and a gentler wind blows the clouds away. Behold, the stars are still there, marching along their appointed paths, untouched and unperturbed by the storm that so recently raged around you. Who put those stars up there? Who keeps them on their courses? Who protects them from the storms that seem so fierce and irresistible? The same God who asks you to have faith in Him.

He created them, and He "bringeth out their host by number: he calleth them all by names by the greatness of his might, for that he is strong in power; not one faileth" (Isaiah 40:26). That was a comforting thought when a sharp eye could count 3,000 stars on the clearest night. How much more comforting it can be to us, now that astronomers estimate a trillion times ten trillion stars plus many more besides. Incredibly, the Bible says God marshals them all by number and calls each one by name! And He's been doing it for billions of years! All-powerful, all-loving, ever-living God. How safely we can trust Him, whatever storm may come!

Watch the birds. Who taught them how to make their nests and where to place them? Who shows them where to find food for their fledglings? Who guides them on their pathless flights? Is it not He who cares so much for little birds that even a sparrow cannot fall to earth without His notice? How assuring, then, to hear Him say that we are worth much more to Him than many sparrows!

Pick a flower. Note the lovely colors of its petals, the sweet perfume, the exquisite arrangement of each part. Why did God make the flowers so attractive, unless He wanted to? Unless He cared? Take a microscope and examine the littlest things He's made. Note the delicate design of every infinitesimal detail.

Surely there is nothing too small for our God to care about, nor too large for Him to protect!

Why is it, then, that when difficulties rear their ugly heads before us, when some sorrow strikes us low, we cry out with the disciples in Galilee's storm, "Carest thou not that we perish?"

Isaiah chides, "Why sayest thou, O Jacob, and speakest, O Israel, My way is hid from the Lord . . . ? Hast thou not known? hast thou not heard, that the everlasting God, the Lord, the Creator of the ends of the earth, fainteth not, neither is weary? there is no searching of his understanding. He giveth power to the faint; and to them that have no might he increaseth strength. Even the youths shall faint and be weary, and the young men shall utterly fall: but they that wait upon the Lord shall renew their strength; they shall mount up with wings as eagles; they shall run, and not be weary; and they shall walk, and not faint" (Isaiah 40:27-31).

Expect Trials

If our faith is to grow to withstand the winds of the final tempest, we must expect difficulties to test us and disappointments to make us strong. Olympic athletes who "go for the gold" expect to spend long years in daily discipline, paining every muscle and demanding of themselves the utmost endurance. These athletes seek—even demand—to enter every competition that will test their progress and give opportunity to demonstrate their growing skills. An athlete who avoids these tests or who gives up after some defeat can never expect to hear his country's anthem played in his honor or feel his fingers grasp the coveted medal. The player who gets the gold learns from his defeats; he asks his coach, How can I do better? He goes back to his practice more determined than before.

Shall we, who seek a golden crown, expect to put out less effort to get it? We have this great advantage, that our Coach knows what we need. With Him to guide us, we shall mount up with wings as eagles, run without weariness, walk and not faint. His athletes have never lost a medal yet. If only we have enough faith in Him to do whatever He tells us, we are sure to win.

Faith From Fulfilled Prophecies

Faith will increase as we study the evidence of fulfilled prophecies. Today's best weathermen can scarcely tell the weather a couple days in advance. Much less can our vaunted news anchormen predict the course of nations. So when we read in the Bible that God has foretold the destiny of empires centuries before those empires existed, and His predictions have been accurately fulfilled, we can have absolute faith that He knows the outcome of the storm that is brewing over our world today.

Faith From Answered Prayer

The Bible contains many accounts of answered prayer; Daniel in the lions' den, Jonah in the whale, Hezekiah pleading for health, the Roman centurion asking that his servant be healed, Jairus begging for his little daughter's life. We can read these true stories, see how God answered, and find our faith growing stronger.

But there is nothing stopping us from testing whether the living God will indeed hear and answer *our* prayers. Quite to the contrary! We are *encouraged* to "come boldly unto the throne of grace, that we may obtain mercy, and find grace to help in time of need" (Hebrews 4:16). God wants us to come to Him so He can help us and so we will know He is our friend.

It can be very exciting, the first time God answers prayer. Uncle Arthur, author of *Uncle Arthur's Bedtime Stories*, used to say again and again, "God loves to answer little children's prayers." Some grown-ups scoffed, but the children who put God to the test find He really does love to answer. Uncle Arthur encouraged children to write and tell him of such answers, and letters came from around the world. After he died, they continued to come, and I have a collection of hundreds.

One letter came from a girl in India who lost a ball. After she and her friends had searched a long time in vain, she gathered them around her and told them that Uncle Arthur said that Jesus loves to answer prayer. She wrote, "I told them we would pray, and that after we had found the ball I would write and tell Uncle Arthur." The little group of children bowed their heads at her direction, prayed, and promptly found the ball. "Now I'm writing you, Uncle Arthur, just as I promised."

Another letter was from a girl in Africa whose mother had given her a rosary with the strict injunction that it not be taken to school. She wrote to say that she took it to school, lost it, searched in vain, prayed, and found it, then wrote Uncle Arthur to report another answered prayer.

A little girl in a hungry family in Loma Linda, California, was overjoyed to report that their prayer for food was promptly answered by a shout outside and a van amply stocked with food from concerned church members.

But perhaps my favorite letter came from Singapore, from a young teenager who admitted she lived in a Hindu home and still prayed to heathen gods. When she failed the matriculation exam so vitally important for ambitious youth studying under the British education system, she bethought herself of *Bedtimes* and that wonderful promise, God loves to answer children's prayers. But would the Christian God hear and answer a heathen girl's request? So devastated was she by the exam results that on a Friday morning she hid behind a partition in her home where her mother could not see her and dared to approach the God of heaven. When she went to school Monday morning, her teacher said she had felt impressed to check her exam again and found she had marked parts of it wrong. The girl had passed! Ecstatically, she wrote Uncle Arthur, "Now I know the Christian God answers prayers of all people everywhere." What a marvelous discovery! And God has other wonders to display to those who pray to Him.

To anyone who has never prayed, let me assure you, He will answer your prayers, too, for He longs for you to love and trust Him. But there is a mistake we must avoid. Some people say that whether God answers prayer depends on how much faith we have. This can be quite misleading. Sometimes He answers prayers because our faith is weak; sometimes, if our faith is strong, He withholds the answer we request to give us something better.

For examples, consider how quickly Jesus answered the prayer of the nobleman whose son was sick. Jesus knew that that man would have given up what little faith he had if he had not gotten exactly what he wanted right away (see John 4:46-53). But when Lazarus was sick and Mary and Martha sent that most trusting message, "He whom thou lovest is sick," Jesus seemed to ignore the request and let Lazarus die.

He wanted to do something much better for Lazarus than merely heal him; He had healed hundreds in the course of His ministry. He wanted to use Lazarus as incontestable proof that He is the Resurrection and the Life, to give hope and comfort to all His faithful people who would lay their loved ones in graves before He returned. But to do so, He had to let Mary and Martha see their brother die and think He didn't care. Four days He waited to prove Lazarus was truly dead. Then He went to Bethany, and what joy there was when Lazarus came forth from the tomb alive (see John 11:1-44)! So if you know you have confessed all your sins and God has not given you what you asked for, be joyful. He has something much better in mind.

Besides all this, in the storm about to engulf us, there will be much to test our faith. Waiting for answers now will make waiting easier then.

Faith From God's Promises

When the storm breaks, it will involve the whole world. No one will escape. But while some will be exposed to the full force of the winds and waves, those who trust God will be shielded by His all-protecting arm. He has promised, and He never breaks a promise. Get acquainted with as many of His promises as you can. They are all through the Bible. Learn them by heart, and they will come to mind to encourage you when you need them most.

Here is a good one. "The Lord also shall roar out of Zion," says the prophet Joel, "and utter His voice from Jerusalem; and the heavens and the earth shall shake: but the Lord will be the hope of His people, and the strength of the children of Israel" (Joel 3:16).

In all the upheaval, the familiar promises of Psalm 91 will take on new meaning.

> He that dwelleth in the secret place of the most High shall abide under the shadow of the Almighty. I will say of the Lord, He is my refuge and my fortress: my God; in him will I trust. Surely he shall deliver thee from the snare of the fowler, and from the noisome pestilence. He shall cover thee with his feathers, and under his wings shalt thou trust: his truth shall be thy shield and buckler. Thou shalt not be afraid for the terror by night; nor for the arrow that flieth by day; nor for the pestilence that walketh in darkness; nor for the destruction that wasteth at noonday. . . . Only with thine eyes shalt thou behold and see the reward of the wicked. Because thou hast made the Lord, which is my refuge, even the most High, thy habitation; there shall no evil befall thee, neither shall any plague come nigh thy dwelling. For he shall give his angels charge over thee, to keep thee (Psalm 91:1-11).

How much evidence God has given on which to base our faith! All who develop the faith of Jesus will anticipate the gathering storm without fear, confident that He will be their "refuge and strength, a very present help" until the storm is over (see Psalm 46:1).

Chapter 9

No More Need for Refuge

(Revelation 14:13-20)

I looked, and behold a white cloud, and upon the cloud one sat like unto the Son of man, having on his head a golden crown, and in his hand a sharp sickle. Revelation 14:14.

John is still watching the "great controversy vision." Observing over his shoulder, we suddenly feel our hearts beat quicker. Muscles tense with mounting excitement. The unfolding vision presents a scene of the utmost interest—the grand, climactic event for which all God's people have yearned with heartfelt longing since that sad evening so long ago when Adam and Eve were thrust from Eden.

There, before us, we see Jesus coming in power and glory, seated on a white cloud, invested with a golden crown and wielding a sharp sickle. A voice calls from heaven, "Thrust in thy sickle, and reap . . . : for the harvest of the earth is ripe."

How Will Jesus Come?

Ask an Adventist, "How will Jesus come?" and the chances are good he'll say, "Sitting on a cloud and surrounded by angels."

"Good," you say. "But can you add to that? Will He have anything special on His head or in His hand?"

"Oh, yes, of course. He'll have a crown and a sickle, won't He?"

"That's right," you say. "Can you tell me more? Will there

be any noise, or will He come silently?"

"Oh, noisily," he says. "There will be lots of noise. Doesn't Paul or somebody say something about a trumpet blast?"

His companion breaks in, "Isn't there something about God shouting? Seems to me I read that somewhere."

"Right again," you say. "Paul said Jesus would descend with a shout, with the voice of the archangel and the trump of God. But now, tell me, will anyone see Him come? Some people talk about a secret rapture, though I understand they just use the word *rapture* nowadays. Will Jesus' coming be secret?"

This time the friend answers first. She says, "There'll be nothing secret about it. Jesus warned His disciples that if anyone says Jesus has come in a secret place, we aren't supposed to believe it."

You smile and congratulate her. Then you challenge them both. "Can you prove that people will actually *see* Jesus come?"

"Oh, yes," he says eagerly. "Let me see—It's in Revelation, isn't it? 'Every eye shall see him, and they also which pierced him.' " He pauses, rather pleased with himself for remembering.

She says, "Let me think. Didn't Jesus—No, no! It was when Jesus was on trial. Caiaphas—he was the high priest, wasn't he? Didn't he command Jesus to say whether He was the Messiah, and didn't Jesus say something like, You will see the Son of man coming in the clouds of heaven? Please tell me I'm right. I'm sure I studied that back in a Bible class in academy."

Yes, she was right, and so was he; in fact, all the answers were right. Adventists are quite well informed about the second coming. It's an interesting subject.

Hundreds of References

In fact, it's so interesting that Bible writers refer to it again and again. Someone has counted more than 300 references to the second coming in the New Testament alone. Each adds something.

For instance, the crown and sickle are mentioned definitely only in our present text, Revelation 14:14. The cloud is referred to often; and angels are frequently associated with the Advent (see Matthew 13:41; 24:31). Statements that Jesus comes *with* the angels occur at the beginning of the "inasmuch" parable (see Matthew 25:31) and in Jesus' answer to His own question, "What shall a man give in exchange for his soul?" (see Matthew 16:26, 27).

The sound of the trumpet is mentioned in Matthew 24:31 and also in 1 Thessalonians 4:16, 17, which adds the shout and the voice of the archangel. The latter text also includes the comforting information that Jesus will raise the faithful dead and gather the righteous living to be with Him on the cloud, "and so shall we ever be with the Lord."

Matthew 24:27 likens the advent to lightning. The statement that "every eye" will see Him occurs in Revelation 1:7, which also hints of a special resurrection before Jesus appears. How else could those who pierced Him see Him come, unless they were restored to life beforehand?

Acts 1:11 assures us that the One who comes will be "this same Jesus" whom the disciples saw go into heaven—the very same gracious, kind, caring Jesus the disciples knew so well and admired so much. He is to come "in like manner" as the disciples saw Him go into heaven. The disciples looked up as they watched Him go; so when the genuine Jesus returns, the inhabitants of earth must look up to see Him come. For that reason, all "christs" who simply appear on earth can be known immediately as false. Jesus said there would be many of them (see Matthew 24:5, 23-26).

Revelation 6:15-17 tells the reaction of the wicked when they see Jesus coming. Panic-stricken kings and servants, rich and poor alike call for the rocks and mountains to fall and hide them.

Matthew 24:30 speaks of "the sign of the Son of man in heaven" but doesn't say what the sign will be. Ellen White identifies it: "Soon there appears in the east a small black cloud, about half the size of a man's hand. It is the cloud which surrounds the Saviour and which seems in the distance to be shrouded in darkness. The people of God know this to be the sign of the Son of man" (*The Great Controversy,* p. 640).

She adds many details, like the words Jesus will use when He calls the righteous dead to life, and how He will reassure the fearful saints. She brings a host of Bible texts together to make the most vivid description yet written of Christ's coming. "God's People Delivered," near the end of *The Great Controversy*, is a thrilling chapter worth reading again and again.

So Adventists have abundant evidence to describe the second coming as we do, with the clouds and the crown, the sickle and the trumpets and the vast angelic host. But if this traditional picture fully describes Christ's return, what should we do with the white horses?

Riders on White Horses

Revelation 19:11-16 gives a totally different view of the Advent! Here we find neither cloud nor sickle, trumpets nor shouts. There are angels, to be sure, but they ride white horses; none fly. Instead of wearing one crown, Jesus has many crowns. The sickle is missing, replaced by a sharp sword that comes out of Jesus' mouth. How can such a totally different picture describe the same event?

Why Different Descriptions?

God has given us descriptions of the second coming in bits and pieces and even in two very different versions, not to confuse us, but simply because His coming will be such a grand, spectacular event that no human being, inspired or otherwise, could ever adequately convey the stupendous impact it will have, both on this world and on all the awe-struck universe.

Consider what happened on May 6, 1937. Fifty years ago, scheduled airline passenger traffic across the Atlantic was still a distant dream. But Germany had built a huge lighter-than-air dirigible that had successfully carried 1,002 passengers over the ocean in ten round-trip flights during 1936 and was about to complete its first westbound flight of the 1937 season. Radio newscasting was still in its infancy, but someone had suggested that so monumental a moment as the mooring of this modern marvel at Lakehurst, New Jersey, was worthy of live network radio coverage—something still unusual in those days. I was in California and heard everything as it developed. And I find there are still a few other gray heads who recall the incident.

At first the announcer calmly described the crowds and the weather. There had been a thunderstorm a little earlier, and there was still some drizzle, though visibility was good. It was after seven in the evening, and twilight was turning on lights here and there. At last the *Hindenburg* came in sight. The announcer described how gracefully it floated toward the mooring mast. Then our startled ears heard him exclaim, "Oh, it's burning! it's burning! Oh, dear! This is terrible! terrible! People are falling to the ground, burning! Oh, it's terrible, it's terrible, it's terrible!" He couldn't go on; someone had to take the microphone from him. I'm quoting from memory after fifty-one years, but those others who remember say I'm not far off.

What had happened was that as the *Hindenburg* approached the mooring mast, something ignited the highly inflammable hydrogen gas that gave the vessel lift. There was a tremendous explosion, and flames began devouring everything in reach. Members of the ground crew dashed to safety; but the ninety-seven passengers and crew were not so fortunate. Some leaped out the windows, some were blown out of them, to be picked up dead, or, if alive, often injured or burned. Others fell to the ground with clothes and bodies flaming. *The New York Times* reported next day twenty-one known dead and twelve more missing.

And the radio reporter couldn't describe it. That's the point. Given the unexpected nature of the accident and the extent of the tragedy, many of us would have had difficulty describing it too. How many times we begin a letter to tell a friend about some event in our daily life, and after a few sentences draw a line and say, "I can't write it all now. There's just too much. I'll have to wait till the next time we get together and tell you then."

On the other hand, this indescribable scene was only one airship burning with a few bodies falling out. So consider what would have happened if God had given John or Paul or any other prophet a full-scale viewing of the actual second coming. Every one of them would have been tongue-tied. They would have gasped, "Lord, I'd love to tell Your people what You've shown me, but where—how—do I begin?"

God didn't want that to happen. He *wants* us to know as much as possible about the second coming. He wants us to tell our friends and neighbors about it, so they will know too.

The Friendly Farmer

So, for example, He showed John the cloud with Jesus sitting on it with a crown and a sickle. John looked carefully and was delighted to see that the distinguished Traveler was the Son of man, his old Friend from those happy days by Galilee. He was wearing a crown, and John understood at once, for his Friend had said He was going to receive a kingdom. And He carried a sickle; John had seen many a farmer with a sickle—he'd probably used one himself on occasion. Jesus had often described the end of the world as a harvest. So good Friend Jesus, crowned King, was returning as He had said He would, to reap the final harvest. "Sure!" we can hear John whisper. "I can write a description of this." He put it all in just one verse that we can easily memorize and long remember.

Just so, God gave other prophets glimpses, which they could describe in a few words that we could understand and master—important when every word had to be copied by hand and people had to rely on their memories because books were scarce.

The longest description by far is Ellen White's. Nowadays, printing presses make copying easy, and abundant books make memorizing less necessary. Besides, Jesus will come in *our* day. It was enough that earlier peoples knew that He would return someday; but for us, this will be the major event of our lives, and God has very kindly given us much more information about it than He gave earlier believers. Even so, He didn't show Ellen White everything, and in her *Great Controversy* description she leaves out choice details she includes in *Early Writings*. In the earlier version, she describes Jesus' hair as white and curly and lying on His shoulders (see page 16). None of this appears in *The Great Controversy*. In *Early Writings*, Jesus wears many crowns; in *The Great Controversy,* a "diadem of glory rests on His holy brow" (page 641). And *Early Writings* says that Jesus has a sharp sickle in His right hand and a silver trumpet in His left. Then this: As the cloud approaches the earth in flames of fire, Jesus plays a trumpet solo. It's a very friendly second coming, almost cozy, as if God designed it to attract the attention of a seventeen-year-old girl and to comfort the fears and fill the loneliness of a small group of faithful believers who had just suffered a great disappointment.

Our Pictures Are Too Small!

But I believe God also wants us to see the second coming for the tremendous event it will be. From the way we talk, strangers might conclude that Adventists consider baseball's World Series much more significant than the second coming. And I confess that we in our publishing houses are somewhat to blame for this. Even splendidly colored renditions of the second coming printed in our finest books and magazines show only fifty or sixty angels at most; and though the front-row angels are fully formed, those in the back rows are increasingly reduced to curves and squiggles. We've done even worse. We've reduced these pictures to fit the width of a column of type—picture two inches wide and an inch and a half high. Why, we've reduced the second coming to the size of a couple of postage stamps! No wonder preachers stammer trying to explain to skeptics how "every eye will see Him." We've heard some say the cloud will travel around the earth, and that's how everyone will see. How relieved some preachers were when television came. Now people on the other side of the world would see Jesus on giant TV screens.

That's why Jesus said to John, "I want you to see another view of My coming."

The Invincible Conqueror

Suddenly John saw heaven opened, and, as he wrote later, "behold a white horse; and he that sat upon him was called Faithful and True, and in righteousness he doth judge and make war. His eyes were as a flame of fire, and on his head were many crowns; and he had a name written, that no man knew, but he himself. And he was clothed with a vesture dipped in blood: and his name is called The Word of God. And the armies which were in heaven followed him upon white horses, clothed in fine linen, white and clean. And out of his mouth goeth a sharp sword, that with it he should smite the nations: and he shall rule them with a rod of iron: and he treadeth the winepress of the fierceness and wrath of Almighty God. And he hath on his vesture and on his thigh a name written, KING OF KINGS, AND LORD OF LORDS" (Revelation 19:11-16).

This was no farmer coming to reap his fields. Here was the mightiest Conqueror of all time. Before John's astonished eyes, Christ's cavalry paraded past, rank upon rank, division after division, army following army, all uniformed in white robes, all riding white horses, all in perfect order. No Roman Ceasar ever commanded a fighting force that could compare with it. Nor did Alexander the Great or Darius the Persian or Nebuchadnezzar of Babylon. And still they came, those multiplied legions, ten thousand times ten thousand of them. Millions upon millions. And more, and still more, from as far as John's straining eyes could see.

Oh, let's stop worrying whether the second coming is big enough to tell our neighbors about. Don't even wonder how the other side of the world will see it too. Jesus is not talking about some petty sideshow. This is that climactic event toward which all history has moved. It is the sublime climax for which the Father and Son have planned these 6,000 years and more. Our old world will be surrounded by the second coming, because the second coming is God's supreme expression of His love, and His love surrounds all.

Alas, those will need a refuge from the second coming who do not fill their hearts with love for Jesus now. But, for those who do, the second coming will be the day when Jesus takes His treasured possessions where there will never be need for a refuge again.

Hasten, glorious day!

Chapter 10

The Dragon Unleashed

(Revelation 15:1–16:21)

Behold, the temple of the tabernacle of the testimony in heaven was opened: . . . and no man was able to enter into the temple, till the seven plagues of the seven angels were fulfilled. Revelation 15:5-8.

After the ecstatic scene of the second coming that closed the fourteenth chapter, it seems almost anticlimactic to wade through the horrors of chapters 15 and 16. But let us remember that that is the view of comfortable Christians who have never suffered persecution, who know the dragon only by his seductive whispers. Those who have experienced the sharpness of his teeth find a good deal of comfort in God's assurance that he will be punished in due time.

John has been faulted for making a muddle out of much of Revelation. The candles and crowns, trumpets and horns, lambs and leopards and locusts and lions, and—especially—the many quick changes of scene, seem to make no sense at all. But those who take time to study the book carefully are amazed to find how well John organized it.

A Major Transition

Chapter 15 marks a major transition. Up to this point, John has reported four major visions that described the history of the Christian church and the world around it from the time of Christ to the close of probation. From chapter 15 on, everything takes place after the close of probation.

For the sake of clarity, there are a few minor exceptions to this rule. But in the main, it is a very helpful rule to keep in mind while reading the book.

Chapters 1 to 14 happen before probation closes.

Chapters 15 and 16 record the close of probation and the ten final plagues, which follow immediately thereafter.

Chapter 17 shows how the plagues affect the great whore, with some allusions to earlier events to explain why she is to be punished so severely.

Chapter 18 describes the effect of the plagues on Babylon, though God's final invitation, "Come out of her, my people," must be announced before the plagues fall, while forgiveness is still available.

Chapter 19 describes the wedding supper of the Lamb, Christ's coming on a white horse, and the feast of the birds—all happening after probation closes.

Chapter 20 belongs later yet, after the second coming, for it describes the millennium and the final elimination of sin.

Chapters 21 and 22 are all about New Jerusalem and the new earth.

So think of chapters 1 to 14 as containing four parallel, historical visions; most of the events they predict have already been fulfilled. Chapters 15 to 22 record end-time events, almost all of which are still in the future.

News From the Temple

Like the first four visions, the vision of the seven last plagues begins with a view of the heavenly temple. In the first view, introducing the letters to the churches, Jesus was walking among the seven candlesticks. In the second, introducing the seals, John saw God's throne surrounded by singing angels. In the third, introducing the trumpets, an angel was ministering at the altar of incense. And in the fourth, at the start of the "great controversy vision," John saw the ark of the testament in the Most Holy Place. All four suggested activity in the temple on behalf of sinners.

But as the fifth vision opens, John sees activity in the temple that forebodes great suffering for sinners. The temple is opened, and out come seven angels carrying seven plagues. One of the four beasts gives the angels seven golden bowls "full of the wrath of God." Then God's glory fills the temple, and sinners can no longer enter.

Because the temple is the place to which penitent sinners must come to confess their sins and receive forgiveness, to be denied access to the temple puts an end to forgiveness. That is why we say that Revelation 15:8 describes the close of probation.

Decision to Close Is Not Arbitrary

In closing probation at this time, God is not being arbitrary; He doesn't say, "You sinners have had your chance and didn't use it; henceforth, I refuse to forgive you." Not at all. He closes probation because everyone on earth has made up his or her mind for righteousness or for evil. The good people, having chosen righteousness, are "without fault before the throne of God"; they have no further need of forgiveness. The rest of earth's inhabitants, having rejected righteousness, see no need for forgiveness and do not ask for it.

The decision to close probation is not so much God's as it is ours.

The Seven Plagues

The plagues are fearsome! What a dreadful list they make! "Grievous sores." Seas and rivers turned to blood. The sun scorching men to death. Darkness over the world. Unprecedented preparations for worldwide warfare. A storm of 100-pound hailstones. An earthquake that sinks islands and swallows mountains.

No wonder all who read about the plagues ask, Are they universal, so that everyone must suffer them? Are they real or symbolic? How long will they last?

There is general agreement that the earlier plagues are not universal, for if they fell on everyone, no one would live long enough to see Jesus come.

Are they real or symbolic? There seems to be a mix of both. Ellen White treats the final earthquake and hailstorm, with the "voices, and thunders, and lightnings" of the seventh plague, as literal (see *The Great Controversy*, pp. 637, 644). The "noisome and grievous sores" of the first plague, likewise, seem literal enough. On the other hand, the "three unclean spirits like frogs" are obviously symbolic.

There is much less certainty about the sea turning into the "blood of a dead man." This may be literal. Or we could be reading John's attempt to describe something he didn't fully understand, as when he speaks of a sea of "glass mingled with fire" and streets of "pure gold, as it were transparent glass" (Revelation 15:2; 21:21). When the redeemed see that sea and walk those streets, they will understand why John described them as he did. We must recognize that, under the second plague, the sea may—or may not—turn into actual blood. But all who see it will agree that John did a good job describing it.

How long will the plagues last? Several texts suggest an answer. Revelation 18:8 says Babylon's "plagues come in one day." Verse 17 says, "one hour." In strict prophetic time, this could be a year or two weeks. Under the fifth plague, sinners still suffer from the sores of the first plague. It seems certain that the plagues won't last long; they are too devastating.

Why Do the Plagues Fall? One View

Why do the plagues fall? Christians have discussed them for centuries, trying to understand. We'll look at two major explanations.

Many good Christians say that God sends the plagues to demonstrate His righteous indignation. Time and again He has come to sinners in love, and they have spurned Him. God has been patient beyond anything sinners deserve; now let them taste the exhaustion of His patience.

These good Christians say that the plagues are punishment dealt out by God to the finally impenitent. Divine mercy is one side of God's love, divine justice is the other side; and justice demands punishment for lawbreaking.

These same good Christians also say that angels rejoice to see evil men and women get the punishment they so richly deserve. They praise God, "Thou art righteous, O Lord, which art, and wast, and shalt be, because thou hast judged thus." They urge God on: "Reward her even as she rewarded you, and double unto her double according to her works. . . . How much she hath glorified herself, and lived deliciously, so much torment and sorrow give her" (Revelation 16:5; 18:6, 7). God is pleased. He sits happily on His throne while the heavenly beings worship Him, "Amen; Alleluia" (Revelation 19:4).

True, it is unusual for God to punish sinners; He would much rather forgive them. But the Bible speaks of His committing a "strange act." Bringing suffering and death to impenitent sinners by pouring the plagues on them is God's strange act.

The plagues are sent by God to emphasize the difference between the righteous and the unrighteous. Some persons whom God judges to be sinners appear to be pretty good people, while some whom He calls righteous don't appear all that good. Now, as the pains of the plagues continue, sinners curse and blaspheme God for their suffering, while the righteous praise God for His lovingkindness. Thus all in heaven and earth are brought to see that God has judged everyone's character correctly.

Most of all, in the opinion of the good Christians who explain the plagues this way, the plagues demonstrate God's great power. He has permitted sinners to afflict His people a long time; now, in love, He shows that He is powerful enough to make sinners suffer for the suffering they have caused. Thus God comes out on top in the end and wins the great controversy.

Why Do the Plagues Fall? Another View

Many good Christians prefer another interpretation of the seven last plagues.

In this view, Satan gets the blame for all the pain and suffering. *The Great Controversy*, p. 614, says:

> When He [God] leaves the sanctuary, darkness covers the inhabitants of the earth. In that fearful time the righteous must live in the sight of a holy God without an intercessor. The restraint which has

> been upon the wicked is removed, and Satan has entire control of the finally impenitent. God's long-suffering has ended. The world has rejected His mercy, despised His love, and trampled upon His law. The wicked have passed the boundary of their probation; the Spirit of God, persistently resisted, has been at last withdrawn. Unsheltered by divine grace, they have no protection from the wicked one. Satan will then plunge the inhabitants of the earth into one great, final trouble. As the angels of God cease to hold in check the fierce winds of human passion, all the elements of strife will be let loose. The whole world will be involved in ruin more terrible than that which came upon Jerusalem of old.

In this view, God's strange act is that He permits sinners to suffer the full consequences of their sins. Because He knows the dreadful effects of sin, He has always protected sinners from most of the ruin and strife that sin leads to. Christians holding this view of the plagues point out that, although God had warned Adam and Eve that sin leads to death, He kept them alive so as to give them a chance to escape death. He has done the same for all sinners. During the plagues, He withdraws this protection. The results are devastating.

In a way, by restraining Satan from carrying out all his evil plans, God has been unfair to him. After probation closes, in fairness to this one who hates Him so much, God removes the restraint. Satan has full permission to do what he wants with the inhabitants of earth. The result will be—to quote Ellen White again—that "the whole world will be involved in ruin more terrible than that which came upon Jerusalem of old." The horrified angels will see more clearly than ever before why God put Satan out of heaven in the first place, and why, in the judgment just completed, He sentenced sinners to remain outside.

It was stated above that God has been unfair to Satan in restraining him. In doing so, God has also been unfair to Himself. Look at it this way. Jesus and Satan are engaged in a great contest. Jesus is determined to win. But simply winning is not enough. Jesus wants the angels to approve of the way He plays. How can He win their plaudits if He always keeps Satan shackled? He must not forever lock Satan's team in the shower room, as it were. He must let Satan have his innings fair and square. So He hands Satan the bat and tells him, "It's all yours, sir." What follows is described in Revelation as the seven last plagues. When the game is over, none will say that Satan lost because God didn't play fair. Satan will lose because of the fiendish way he throws the bats and balls around and roughs up the players of both teams. Jesus will get all the laurels, not only for winning, but especially for the gracious, sportsmanlike, gentlemanly way He has treated the opposition.

The Bible says the plagues are poured out by angels of God. This is a legitimate objection to the second view. Let's look at it. We are not trying to win an argument, just find the truth.

If all the plagues come from God, then God and the devil are punishing the earth at the same time. This doesn't sound likely.

Moreover, if all the plagues come from God, the governments of earth aren't so far wrong in blaming Sabbath keepers for them.

Where do the three frogs of the sixth plague come from? Does God send them out to deceive the kings of the earth? Certainly not.

Since we can be sure Satan has charge of the three frogs, why is he not involved in the other plagues?

Ellen White says, "A single angel destroyed all the first-born of the Egyptians. . . . The same destructive power exercised by holy angels when God commands, will be exercised by evil angels when He permits. There are forces now ready, and only waiting the divine permission, to spread desolation everywhere" (*The Great Controversy*, p. 614).

There are many forces available to Satan to bring about the bloodlike seas and rivers. Pollution has almost done this already. Nuclear weapons let loose without restraint, chemical and biological poisons released in large quantities, droughts and floods and pestilences—over which Satan already has some control—could easily produce most of the devastating effects described in Revelation 16.

The seventh plague appears at first to be an exception. Nevertheless, the earthquake is a result of sin. Note how much of your hair is pulled into disarray by static electricity in your comb. In the final earthquake, the elements of our decaying world simply react to the highly charged glory of God when Jesus comes to claim His own. When the world was new, it didn't shake while Jesus visited with Adam and Eve. A couple thousand years later, Mount Sinai trembled at God's presence. After six thousand years of sin, it is proper to expect a much more violent response.

In this second way of explaining the plagues:

The seven last plagues demonstrate God's power by revealing the tremendous strength of the evil forces He has kept in check all these years.

The seven last plagues demonstrate God's mercy by the fact that He restrained these forces to give men and women time to receive salvation.

The seven last plagues demonstrate God's love by showing the full measure of the malice Jesus took on Himself when He died on Calvary.

The seven last plagues demonstrate God's generosity. By restraining Satan, Jesus made His opponent look much better than he would otherwise have while men and angels were choosing between them.

The seven last plagues demonstrate God's justice, because God lets sinners suffer only the consequences of their own choices—nothing less, to be sure, but nothing more.

The seven last plagues demonstrate, above all, the wonderful kindness of God because, while sinners were ignorantly glorying in their sins, Jesus gave up everything to save them from the sure results He knew they would otherwise suffer.

No wonder Jesus wins the great controversy!

Oh, for a Refuge!

However we should understand the plagues, whether the first way or the second way or some other way, let's not lose our souls arguing about them, or we'll never find the right answer.

This much is certain. Sinners will wish to be protected from the plagues, but they will wish in vain. Those who have found Jesus to be a tower of strength in times of peace will be oh so very glad for the refuge He will provide them while the plagues fall.

Chapter 11

"Come Out, . . . My People"

(Revelation 17:1–18:24)

I heard another voice from heaven, saying, Come out of her, my people, that ye be not partakers of her sins, and that ye receive not of her plagues. Revelation 18:4.

One can't help wondering how much of Revelation the early Christians understood. How much did John understand as he wrote it? We have difficultly interpreting some of the fulfilled prophecies. For early Christians, practically every fulfillment was still future.

Chapter 17 poses problems for experienced theologians. Who was the beast that "was, and is not; and shall ascend out of the bottomless pit, and go into perdition"? Who are the "seven kings" of whom "five are fallen, and one is, and the other is not yet come"? Where is the "wilderness" where the fallen woman sits?

Chapter 18 records the mysterious, threefold dirge of the kings, the merchants, and the shipmasters, each group in order crying, "Alas, alas," as they bewail the destruction of mystic Babylon (verses 10, 16, 19).

Perhaps those early Christians understood more than we think. At the least, they must have caught the repeated assurance from God that He intended to conquer the dragon and share His unqualified victory with His "treasured possession." As for the beast, despite his vaunted power, he would go into perdition. And though the ten kings would fight the Lamb, the

Lamb would overcome them. How the hearts of those persecuted saints must have quickened with joy to read that the Lamb would call them His "chosen and faithful" followers.

These prophecies can cheer us also. They offer us absolute confidence that God will win the final conflict. In spite of our many failings, if we continue to follow Him, He will call us "chosen and faithful" too.

The Fallen Woman

The early Christians must have noticed the way the "great whore" was dressed. Modern Hollywood directors don't even claim to be Christians, yet they know that pure, Christian women dress very differently from the women of the world, and they dress their actresses accordingly.

Today's TV actress playing the part of a bought woman dresses in suggestive clothing and decks herself with "gold and precious stones and pearls"; bracelets, necklaces, rings, and earrings mark the woman whose heart is far from God. But see how Hollywood dresses a Christian woman, in simplicity and modesty. Like the pure woman of Revelation 12:1, her beauty glows with a heavenly light that clearly outshines the plastic packaging of the prostitute.

In dressing the pure woman and the fallen woman the way He did in Revelation 12:1 and 17:4, 5, was God saying something to His church about the way He wants His people to dress? If Hollywood can see a difference, should Christians be blind? In this day, when we are warned against allowing the ways of the world to invade the church, are Adventist men and women careful to dress the way God wants us to?

"Come Out, . . . My People"

The members of the church in Nazareth grew angry when Jesus said there were many widows in Israel in the days of Elijah, and that the prophet was sent to none of them, but to a widow of "Sarepta, a city of Sidon." When He added that there were many lepers in Israel in the days of Elisha, but only the Syrian, Naaman, was healed, their anger exceeded their self-control. Rising in wrath, they led Jesus to the top of a cliff, intending to hurl Him headlong. Only a miracle saved Him.

Again and again, Jesus tried to get the message across to the Israelites that there were many people "out there" that He wanted "in here." He's telling us the same thing today. "My people" are out there, He says to us, and He's looking to us to help Him bring them in.

Attending Sabbath School and church every Sabbath morning as all good Adventists do, for several years our family had to pass a shopping mall on the way home. Many times our little girls would ask, "How come all those people are shopping on Sabbath, Daddy?" I usually said, "They don't love Jesus very much." It was a simple answer for two very little girls. It was also snobbish; how long I would have gotten away with it, I don't know. But it happened that circumstances brought our children into close friendship with several of those shoppers, especially some Baptists among them, and we discovered that they loved Jesus very much. In fact, they taught our daughters several things about witnessing for our Saviour that they might never have learned from us Adventists.

For fifteen years I corresponded with a minister in India. He wrote first, asking me for *Signs of the Times*. Often over the years he told me he was praying for me and asked me to pray for him. "It's so hard getting the people interested in Jesus here," He wrote after one move. That minister was a Roman Catholic priest. He died recently. His successor has requested that I send him *Signs* by air so copies will arrive sooner. (I do; wouldn't you?) His latest letter requests additional religious literature to display in the archbishop's house for visiting priests to read. He has easy access to the archbishop's house. He is the vicar-general in that archbishopric.

Jesus said, "Other sheep I have, which are not of this fold: them also I must bring." What a thrill it is to correspond with some of them! But Jesus wants them closer than the mailbox! He says, "They shall hear my voice; and there shall be one fold, and one shepherd" (John 10:16). They are already listening to His voice. Many have found the true fold. And before probation closes and the plagues begin, many more will leave the churches they currently attend, to be gathered into that one great fold that Jesus shepherds.

Babylon Finally Fallen

In 1844, the Millerites preached that by rejecting the message of the coming judgment and Christ's return, the popular churches fulfilled the second angel's message, "Babylon is fallen." In *The Great Controversy*, page 389, Ellen White said that while the churches that constitute Babylon had "experienced a moral fall," the "fall was not complete" at that time. But now, as probation is about to close, the angel of Revelation 18:5 says that Babylon's "sins have reached unto heaven, and God hath remembered her iniquities." Ellen White comments, "She has filled up the measure of her guilt, and destruction is about to fall upon her. But," she hastened to add, "God still has a people in Babylon; and before the visitation of His judgments these faithful ones must be called out" (*The Great Controversy*, p. 604).

As God sent angels to call Lot's family from Sodom the night before it was burned up; as God sent Jeremiah to tell the Jews to leave Jerusalem before Nebuchadnezzar's soldiers smashed through its walls; as Jesus warned the Christians to leave Jerusalem when they should see the city encompassed by armies; so now God is sending the Adventists to call His people out of Babylon before the apostate churches are destroyed in the seven last plagues.

Lot's wife lingered, and turned to a pillar of salt. The king and his councilors put Jeremiah down a muddy well, then were captured and tortured trying to race from Jerusalem through a back gate, too late. The Christians fled the capital city as Jesus had told them to and totally escaped the famine, the diseases, the conflagration, and the multiplied thousands of crucifixions that were the final end of the scoffers who relied on false prophets instead of on Christ.

As probation lingers, all of God's true people will leave the churches of Babylon and be gathered into the one true fold.

But how will they recognize that one true fold? More on this in a minute.

The Earth Lightened With Glory

Jesus has a problem! He wants to close probation as soon as the judgment is finished. He also wants to give everyone an equal opportunity to decide for or against Him. How can He meet both objectives?

Here's how. Since it is His Spirit that leads sinners to repentance (see John 16:8-10), He will provide a much-greater-than-usual outpouring of His Spirit as time grows short. Joel described Christ's plan this way, quoting Him: "It shall come to pass afterward, that I will pour out my spirit upon all flesh." At those times, he added, "Whosoever shall call on the name of the Lord shall be delivered: for *in mount Zion and in Jerusalem* shall be deliverance, as the Lord hath said, and in *the remnant* whom the Lord shall call" (Joel 2:28, 32, emphasis supplied).

In his famous sermon at Pentecost, Peter recognized that the first fulfillment of Joel's prophecy was taking place right there on Mount Zion in Jerusalem on that very day (see Acts 2:17-21). A few weeks later he explained that the second fulfillment—when the Spirit will be poured upon the remnant—will occur just before Jesus returns (see Acts 3:19-21).

Jesus amazed the disciples by telling them, "This gospel of the kingdom shall be preached in all the world for a witness unto all nations; and then shall the end come" (Matthew 24:14).

Adventists are still amazed! How will that prophecy be fulfilled? By one estimate, some 270,000 children are born into the world every day. The Adventist church rejoices when, on a rare Sabbath carefully prepared for, our pastors baptize 1,000 in a day. As Andrew said about the little boy's loaves and fishes, "What are they among so many?" (John 6:9). We simply aren't making a very big dent on the world's population. Does this mean we should stop preaching that Christ is coming soon? No!

Did anyone say that all last-day evangelizing will be done by Adventists? Let's hope not. Others are already helping prepare the world for Christ's coming. Here are some examples:

At the council of the United Bible Societies held in

Budapest last September, 272 delegates from 109 countries unanimously pledged themselves and their national Bible societies to provide Bibles and New Testaments in languages they can read to all of the 450,000,000 new Christians they hope will join Christian churches by the year 2000. No Adventist publishing house could begin to provide that many Bibles—and we won't have to; other Christians will.

At the invitation of a neighbor, I attended a Mennonite revival meeting. The little church was jammed, men and boys on one side, women and girls on the other. A deacon led me to the one remaining seat, right in front of the pulpit. The evangelist's topic, believe it or not, was Matthew 24 and the signs of Jesus' coming. Adventists were not invited to preach to those Mennonites, but a Mennonite evangelist preached them an Adventist sermon.

As a denomination, we tend to think we are the only people God can trust to give His message. Do we suffer from Elijah's disease? God tactfully told Elijah that He had 7,000 other faithful servants. If that ratio holds good today—7,000 faithful servants in other churches for every faithful Adventist—God won't lack for servants to give His final message.

God is willing, even eager, to use every Adventist who is willing and eager to help Him give the final message. He has given us so much, blessed us in so many ways, revealed to us so much of His love, that we have so much more to tell than others do. But if we don't want to tell what we know, He'll find others who will tell what they know, and we'll lose the blessing.

Ellen White is very encouraging. She wrote, "The angel who unites in the proclamation of the third angel's message is to lighten the whole earth with his glory. A work of world-wide extent and unwonted power is here foretold" (*The Great Controversy*, p. 611).

Visitors returning from China report that that vast land is more open to Christianity today than ever before. The Communist period weakened many traditions, so that millions are looking for a new faith to replace the old. This fact, coupled with the rough treatment of Christians by the Red Guard, has stirred up a great surge of sympathy for Christianity there.

Look at the unbelievable opportunities for evangelism in Russia! Read the reports from Africa appearing in *Adventist Review*! God is going to find ways to get His message out—and quicker than we may be ready for.

There will be spiritual power enough and to spare. "The great work of the gospel is not to close with less manifestation of the power of God than marked its opening" (*ibid*).

We may expect our publications and radio programs and telecasts to announce God's last invitation. They will help. Laymen may feel they can't give Bible studies well enough to be effective, but that's not God's thinking:

> Servants of God, with their faces lighted up and shining with holy consecration, will hasten from place to place to proclaim the message from heaven. By thousands of voices, all over the earth, the warning will be given. . . . The message will be carried not so much by argument as by the deep conviction of the Spirit of God. The arguments have been presented. The seed has been sown, and now it will spring up and bear fruit. The publications distributed by missionary workers have exerted their influence, yet many whose minds were impressed have been prevented from fully comprehending the truth or from yielding obedience. Now the rays of light penetrate everywhere. . . . Notwithstanding the agencies combined against the truth, a large number take their stand upon the Lord's side (*ibid.*, p. 612).

Which Fold to Join?

They will stand on the Lord's side. They will join the Shepherd's flock. But here is a question every Adventist must ponder. When God's people come out of the other churches, will they be attracted to the Adventist church? Will they feel that our church is God's true fold?

Are our congregations so loving that these new members will feel welcome? Do we obey God's commandments joyfully? Do we live the Adventist lifestyle happily? Do we respect and obviously appreciate the counsels of the testimony of Jesus? Is the name of Jesus often on our lips? Is His faith in our hearts? Is His coming the ultimate goal of all our plans?

We, too, must be God's people. We, too, must join the heavenly Shepherd's flock. For be sure of this, it will be Jesus' fold that God will protect in the persecuting storm so clearly predicted in prophecy.

Chapter 12
Coming Certainly, Coming Soon!
(Revelation 19:1-21)

He saith unto me, Write, Blessed are they which are called unto the marriage supper of the Lamb. Revelation 19:9.

After four chapters of almost undiluted gloom, Revelation 19 brings welcome relief. The opening verses burst with joy. Angels and elders praise God for His superb handling of unrepentant sinners. Joyfully they announce the wedding of Jesus and invite the righteous to come dine with them at the great "marriage supper of the Lamb."

Heaven opens. Jesus sallies forth, riding a white horse. The mounted armies of heaven follow in close order behind Him. Kings and captains muster the legions of earth to resist. One titanic battle engages both sides in a cataclysmic struggle to the death, but the outcome is clear and unequivocal. With the sword of His mouth, Jesus smites the nations. He and His hosts emerge from the contest unscathed and supreme.

The vast armies of the wicked lie dead upon the field. Wild birds flock to eat their still bodies. Their spiritual organizations burn in the sulfurous flames of a lake of fire. Jesus reigns over His loyal, happy people, henceforth and forevermore, the undisputed KING OF KINGS, AND LORD OF LORDS.

How Long Till Supper?

In her youth, Ellen White wrote of John's visions as if they would be fulfilled immediately. Adventist pioneers expected to see the Lord come in their lifetime; they believed the Lamb's marriage supper would be served in the next few months—even within the next few hours. There was much excitement about getting ready for an event so soon to take place.

All that was nearly 150 years ago. The excitement has faded. Some Adventists still look forward eagerly to the second coming. They modify their plans in confident expectation that Jesus will be here soon. Others plan as if His coming were a long way off. They wonder whether perhaps the pioneers were naive, their excitement mistaken.

The Bible has a ready answer. Paul wrote, "Now is our salvation nearer than when we [first] believed" (Romans 13:11). Jesus said, "Watch . . . for ye know not what hour your Lord doth come." He cautioned the disciples, "Be ye also ready: for in such an hour as ye think not the Son of man cometh." "Watch," He repeated, "lest coming suddenly he find you sleeping" (Matthew 24:42-44; Mark 13:35, 36).

If Jesus' coming was near in 1844, it is 145 years nearer today. If daily preparedness was advisable then, how much more appropriate it is now. If there was reason for excitement then—and there was!—there is a hundredfold greater reason for excitement now. As the popular chorus says it so well, Jesus is "coming certainly, coming soon!"

Make no mistake about it; "Your redemption draweth nigh." His coming "is near, even at the doors" (Luke 21:28; Matthew 24:33). "The morning light is breaking, / The darkness disappears." So, do what Jesus commanded! "Lift up your heads"! (Psalm 24:7). Be excited!

Certainty From the Exodus

There is a remarkable similarity between Israel's anticipation of the Exodus and our expectation of the second coming.

In those days it was generally known among the Israelite slaves that God had promised to rescue His people from bondage and lead them to food and freedom in the Promised Land. For four hundred years, faithful parents taught their sons and daughters to repeat God's promise to Abraham.

"Know of a surety," God had told Abraham, "that thy seed shall be a stranger in a land that is not theirs, and shall serve them; and they shall afflict them four hundred years; and also that nation, whom they shall serve, will I judge: and afterward shall they come out with great substance. And thou shalt go to thy fathers in peace; thou shalt be buried in a good old age. But in the fourth generation they shall come hither again" (Genesis 15:13-16). No doubt many an Israelite could repeat the divine promise from memory.

So let's visit the Israelite slaves six months before the Exodus. We expect to find them talking happily of their upcoming emancipation and planning excitedly for their trip to the Promised Land. Travelers from Palestine are pressed into addressing large crowds of joyous slaves eager to learn about the land they will inherit within less than a year.

To our surprise, this is not what we find at all! These Israelites slaves, so soon to be free, are sunk down in gloom and discouragement. Mention of their release brings wry smiles and outright scoffing.

We turn to some of the young people. "Aren't you happy you'll soon be free? What kind of homes are you planning in the Promised Land?"

They look at us contemptuously. "Free!" they sneer. "Who's going to free us from the Egyptians? They've got the biggest army on earth. They are the world's richest nation. And besides, there's a desert out there. It's desert all the way to Palestine. How are we going to cross that?"

"But what about the prophecies?" we say.

They're not listening. They're hurrying to work. One, a little more courteous than the rest, calls over his shoulder, "Slave masters whip late-arrivers hard."

So we turn to a small group of older men apparently too weak or crippled for the slave drivers to bother with. "Are you happy you'll soon be free?"

The question seems to embarrass them. One says, "We don't talk much about it anymore."

"Why not?" we ask. "God promised to free you, and the time is nearly fulfilled."

"Well, you see," the talkative one volunteers, "there was a lot of excitement back a ways. Oh, I'd say it was about eighty—maybe seventy—years ago, now. You see, there was this boy that the princess adopted into the royal family. When we heard he'd gone to live in the palace, we were all sure he was going to lead us out of Egypt. In fact, some of our people had visions. Angels told them he would free us. Let's see. What was that young man's name? I used to know it like I know my own."

Someone suggests, "Moshaw, wasn't it?"

"No!" Another scorns him. "It was Moses."

"That's right, of course," the talkative one agrees. "Moses. How could I forget! He got called that on account of he was drawn up out of the Nile from a basket. Well, I tell you, if you want to talk about excitement, there was excitement back then when our leaders had those visions [see *Patriarchs and Prophets*, p. 245]. We thought our deliverance was right upon us. But Moses tried to get a revolution started and totally failed. Barely escaped the country with his life. His mentor and protector, the princess, just disappeared. We never have found out what happened to her. But with her gone, I tell you, our slavery went from bad to worse to simply frightful. As for Moses and all the big plans about his leading us to freedom, polite people don't talk about them anymore. No one's really sure where he is or what he's doing, though some say he's in Midian herding sheep. The rest of us just figure this slavery's going to go on and on, and the less said about freedom the better. It really riles up the slavers to hear us talk about it."

"But," we object, "what about the four hundred years?"

"Yeah, what about them?" a grumpy one answers. "Some say it's four hundred thirty years. So where do you start counting and how far do you go? It's too confusing for me."

We answer slowly, "If you count the four hundred years from Isaac's weaning, when Abraham was 105 and the son of the heathen woman began hardtiming Abraham's son, you come to this very year we're living in. And if you count the 430 years from God's call to Abraham to come out of Ur when he was 75, you also come to this very year we're living in.

"And," we continue, though it's hard to tell if anyone is listening, "if you count the generations, we are in the fourth generation right now."

"How do you figure that?" says the talkative one. So apparently he was listening.

"Easy," we say. "Levi and all his brothers came into Egypt. That was the first generation. Levi's sons were Gershon, Kohath, and Merari. That's the second generation. Kohath's sons were Amram and Izhar and Hebron and Uzziel. That's the third generation. Amram's sons were Aaron and Moses. That's the fourth generation. And if Moses leads you out, as I believe he will, you have the four generations exactly as the prophecy predicted" (see Exodus 6:16-20).

"Sounds good," says the talkative one.

"Wish we could believe it," says another.

The group breaks up to go about their various tasks. We call after them, "Trust the prophecies! God will fulfill them! You'll see!"

Out on Time

And God did fulfill those prophecies, even though the outlook at the time was so negative. Egypt was the richest nation on earth and the most powerful. The slaves were right when they said no power on earth could free them. Six months before the Exodus, the world situation looked as if Israelite slavery would go on another hundred years at least.

But in those six months—give or take a few weeks, perhaps—God brought Moses back from the sheep, shamed Egypt's religious hierarchy, bankrupted Egypt's finances, squashed Egypt's political organizations, destroyed Egypt's agriculture, smashed Egypt's army—and got Israel out on time, right to the very day predicted in prophecy. Greatly impressed, Moses wrote, "It came to pass at the end of the four hundred and thirty years, even the selfsame day it came to pass, that all the hosts of the Lord went out from the land of Egypt. It is a night to be much observed" (Exodus 12:41, 42).

We Christians leave that night for the Jews to observe at Passover. If we would observe it ourselves every time we are discouraged, it would rebuild our faith in God and our confidence that Jesus is coming soon—just as the prophecies say He will.

Confirmation From Calvary

The disciples spent the Sabbath of crucifixion weekend trembling in the closet, as it were. How different that day would have been if they had believed the prophecies!

Ellen White points out that pilgrims to the Passover brought their sick from many miles away, hoping Jesus would cure them at the feast. They crowded the temple doorway, calling for the Great Healer. Angry priests and rulers told them to be gone, for the Healer was dead. How sadly those poor people retraced their painful steps.

Why weren't the disciples out there at the temple, telling the people to bring their sick to the tomb the next morning? They could have, couldn't they? Hadn't Jesus given them a complete list of prophecies leading up to His death and resurrection, and hadn't every one but the last been fulfilled?

The disciples could have spent Sabbath going up and down the streets of Jerusalem announcing, "Jesus said the priests would arrest Him, and they did.

"He said He would be condemned, and He was.

"He said the soldiers would scourge Him, and they did.

"He said He would be crucified, and He was.

"He said He would die, and He did.

"And, mark this carefully, all of you, He said that on the third day He would rise again, AND HE WILL! Come out to the tomb tomorrow morning and see Him return to life. Bring your sick and injured. He will heal them. Bring your problems and your worries. He will solve them. Bring your sins and bad habits. He will forgive them and give you victory over them all. Come, every one of you. Come! Come! Come!"

If only they had done that, instead of trembling under their blankets! Of all the days they didn't need to fear the priests, that was the day of days. The priests were over at Pilate's office begging for a hundred soldiers to protect them from the disciples. Oh, but that was a day for the disciples to be preaching! I tell you, there would have been a hundred thousand people out there that Easter morning to see the resurrection, and what a start that would have given the Christian church! Thousands upon thousands would have taken the stupendous news home with them. The gospel of Jesus would have gone to earth's remotest bounds within weeks of that glorious Sunday morning!

But the disciples didn't believe. The resurrection was seen by a handful of pagan soldiers who willingly took bribes to say it hadn't happened. It was seven weeks before the Christian church got started, and only 5,000 were converted that day.

If only the disciples had believed the prophecies!

If only!

What a difference it would have made.

We Have Prophecies Too!

We have more prophecies pointing to the return of Christ than the disciples had pointing to the resurrection. We have far more prophecies than God gave the Israelite slaves.

Then why aren't we out telling everyone that Jesus is coming, certainly and soon?

Riding on a white horse He will come, followed by the armies of heaven, to take His people to the marriage supper of the Lamb, where He will be Chief Server. What an invitation we can extend.

Let us review the prophecies much more than we do. Review how remarkably they have been fulfilled. It will help us have faith to believe that Jesus will truly be that impregnable refuge He has promised in the storm that's gaining strength around us right now, and that He will deliver us out of it.

Chapter 13

The Next Thousand Years

(Revelation 20:1-15)

Blessed and holy is he that hath part in the first resurrection: on such the second death hath no power, but they shall be priests of God and of Christ, and shall reign with him a thousand years. Revelation 20:6.

Few topics in the Bible have caught the public fancy or been subjected to so much speculation as the millennium.

Will it happen before Christ comes or after? Will it be spent in heaven or on earth? Or is it merely symbolic and will never really happen?

The account of the millennium really begins in Revelation 19:11, with the coming of Jesus on the white horse. It continues through the destruction of the wicked and the re-creation of the earth, ending in Revelation 21:8.

There is only one possible time for the millennium: It has to begin when Jesus comes. There is only one place where the saints can be, and that is in heaven. The wicked are dead, all of them.

Why Have the Millennium?

The judgment is over. The final destiny of humans and angels has been forever fixed. So why not move forward at once? Sin will never rise again; God has promised. So light the fire! Burn the wicked! Get rid of Satan! Let righteousness reign supreme! Re-create the world! Give the saints full enjoyment of their inheritance *now*! Why wait longer?

Why wait *a thousand years*?

Everything in the Bible must be looked at in terms of the great controversy between Christ and Satan and God's determination that sin will not arise a second time. There are still a few questions left that, if not answered now, could cause trouble later. We can think of some.

Did God decide *every* case right? Has He condemned some who should have been saved, or brought some to heaven who should have been left out?

What about the millions who lived before Calvary? The heathen? All others who were told little or nothing about Christ and salvation? Has Christ dealt fairly with them?

A Time for Saints to Judge

John tells us that the saints will judge. He says he "saw thrones, and they sat upon them, and judgment was given unto them." They will go through the records and see why loved ones are not in heaven with them. This will answer any questions they may have in regard to God's dealings with those they have held most dear.

And they will work with Jesus in deciding how much punishment the impenitent deserve. This will forever remove any danger that some might question whether God was too severe with sinners, or too lenient. Reviewing what she saw in one of her early visions, Ellen White described the process vividly (see *Early Writings*, p. 291).

A Time for Satan to Worry

The thousand years will be a time for Satan and his angels to tremble in terror, contemplating the fate that awaits them when the millennium ends. They walk about the darkened earth, observing the ruin they have wrought—tumbled buildings, broken bridges, empty factories, smashed airplanes, fruitless orchards, deserted crop land, rusting autos, leering skulls of lifeless corpses.

Self-condemned by whatever residue of rationality he still retains, Satan is also accused and criticized by the grumbling gangs he goaded to rebel. Taught by his own malice to disobey and cheat the God of love, his legions give him little now but disobedience and disloyalty. What a miserable period the millennium will be for him.

A Time for Proof

The thousand years is a time for Satan to prove he can create a world and organize its inhabitants in a happy, prosperous state. At the beginning of the great controversy, he complained when he was left out of the divine committee that planned our earth. It was on this point that the great controversy first broke out. "I saw that when God said to his Son, Let us make man in our image, Satan was jealous of Jesus. He wished to be consulted concerning the formation of man" (*Spiritual Gifts*, vol. 1, p. 17). It is fitting that the great controversy finish where it started, with Satan given unhindered opportunity to prove that he can create a world as good as the one Jesus created six thousand years ago.

Satan is bound in the "bottomless pit" (Revelation 20:1). The Greek word for "bottomless pit" is the Greek word for "deep" in Genesis 1:2, where the world before Creation is described by the phrase, "darkness was upon the face of the deep." Six thousand years ago, Jesus looked upon the darkened deep and said, "Let there be lights," and there were lights. He said, "Let there be a firmament." "Let the waters . . . be gathered . . . and let the dry land appear." "Let us make man in our image" (Genesis 1:3-26). To every command of Jesus, the deep responded obediently; Jesus "spake, and it was done; he commanded, and it stood fast" (Psalm 33:9).

For six thousand years, Satan persuaded men and women to attribute creation to idols or to natural forces or—in our scientific age—to blind chance guided by "natural selection." Certainly, in his version, creation didn't need Jesus. Now he has opportunity to exert his creative powers on the same "darkened deep" on which Jesus worked so successfully.

Satan said that his laws were much better than God's, that his great goal was to improve the statutes of Jehovah (see *The*

Great Controversy, p. 498). How very fair of God to give him a thousand years to prove his claims, to show that he can create a world as good as the one Jesus created, and to fill it with inhabitants even more kind, more generous, more loving than the angels that inhabit heaven. No wonder, when the millennium is over and Satan has failed on both claims, saints and angels will praise God for His justice and mercy. Even to His archenemy, He has ben supremely gracious.

The thousand years will also give time to prove that Jesus was right in taking to heaven some whom the angels question—youth who died before their characters were fully formed, men and women from heathen lands who never heard the name of Christ, autistic and hyperactive persons whose ugly deeds were traceable to conditions about which they were ignorant or over which they had no control. For a thousand years the angels watch these less-favored humans and discover that they fit into heaven perfectly. Jesus was right. They were safe to save.

God knows that the one sure defense against sin is evidence—evidence of the terrible consequences of sin compared to the beauty and peace and contentment of love. He intends there shall be enough evidence to ward off sin forever.

The Millennium Ends

As the thousand years draw to a close, Jesus descends with the saints, and New Jerusalem settles onto the earth. The wicked are raised to life with the same diseases and deformities with which they died. Satan sets to work at once to consolidate their allegiance. He tells them that he resurrected them. He heals them and then, no doubt, gets them busy building huge apartment complexes and factories, repairing bridges and roads, plowing fields, erecting hospitals and prisons. Probably many prisons, for the master lawbreaker generates lawlessness.

New Jerusalem sits on the site of old Jerusalem, resplendent in the glory of God, its gates wide open for passersby to see the beauty of its golden streets and the radiant happiness of its peaceful citizens. Satan tells the resurrected sinners that they deserve to be there, that it is only Jesus who keeps them out, and that it is his intention to win the city for them. He assures them that, if they will attack the city as he directs, they will soon be inside, enjoying all the pleasures Christ denies them.

Sinners who once read Revelation know the plan is doomed, but what other chance have they? Other sinners, already in the habit of believing Satan's lies, believe him now. Perhaps, too, some resurrected preachers of apostate churches assure them that when God sees how much they want inside, He will forgive them in love and permit them to enter.

Plans finally completed, sinners fully trained and armed, Satan gathers his troops "together to battle: the number of whom is as the sand of the sea. And," John tells us, "they went up on the breadth of the earth, and compassed the camp of the saints about, and the beloved city" (Revelation 20:8, 9). Jesus orders the gates closed.

With what intense interest John must have watched these unfolding scenes. Now, as the city is about to be attacked, John says, "I saw a great white throne, and him that sat on it. . . . And I saw the dead, small and great, stand before God; and the books were opened: and another book was opened, which is the book of life: and the dead were judged out of those things which were written in the books, according to their works" (Revelation 20:11, 12).

The Final Judgment

To the accompaniment of the marvelous melodies of heaven's finest choirs, Jesus is crowned in the presence of every soul who ever drew breath in heaven or on earth. Then the final judgment begins.

"As soon as the books of record are opened, and the eye of Jesus looks upon the wicked, they are conscious of every sin which they have ever committed" (*The Great Controversy*, p. 666). They remember the first steps they took in sin. They recall the times their parents or a church school teacher or a pastor pleaded with them to let Jesus bring them victory. They sit again in church or chapel and hear week of prayer sermons and relive altar calls when they scoffed at the strong urging of God's spirit, and they will admit that God has done everything possible to save them from this day.

Then, Ellen White tells us, "above the throne is revealed the cross; and like a panoramic view appear the scenes of Adam's temptation and fall, and the successive steps in the great plan of redemption" with special emphasis on the closing scenes of Christ's sacrifice (*The Great Controversy*, pp. 666, 667).

When that presentation is over, will Jesus make an altar call? Will He plead with the sinners outside the city to come forward, even at this late date, and ask Him to bring their lives into conformity with His will? It would certainly be in harmony with His character to do so.

This we do know, that Jesus' presentation of the plan of salvation, there at the end of the millennium, will be more eloquent than the most persuasive sermon ever preached by the world's most effective evangelists. If any appeal to repentance can reach the hearts of the sinners outside the city, that sermon will. The saints inside will be heartbroken to realize afresh that their salvation was bought at the cost of Jesus' death; they will "raise a song of praise that echoes and reechoes through the vaults of heaven: 'Salvation to our God which sitteth upon the throne, and unto the Lamb' " (*ibid.*, p. 665).

But among the sinners outside, not one will respond. Satan has deceived the world into thinking that God keeps sinners out of heaven. Nothing could be further from the truth. Sinners keep themselves out. Character is a lot like concrete. When first mixed, concrete is soft and pliable and can be molded to almost any shape the builder desires. But once it sets, concrete is one of the hardest of substances; it can be chipped or broken, but it can never again be molded. Ellen White speaks of the character development of the righteous as "a settling into the truth, both intellectually and spiritually, so they cannot be moved" (*SDA Bible Commentary*, vol. 4, p. 1161). Sinners, likewise, will be fully set in their ways, and nothing—not even the most eloquent presentation by time's most effective Preacher—will be able to change them. That is why, however urgently Jesus may appeal, they will have no second probation.

The End of the Wicked

Alas, it is all too true that Jesus can do nothing more to save the sinners assembled "over the breadth of the earth." All, wherever they lived, whenever they lived, have now heard the story of salvation. Yet, even in the full light of the cross, they have no intention of bringing their lives into conformity with God's will. The angels are satisfied that Jesus has been abundantly fair with them. All their questions have been answered. There is no need to continue the controversy longer. So, John tells us, "fire came down from God out of heaven, and devoured them" (Revelation 20:9).

What kind of fire this will be is an intriguing question to which we may not know the answer till we ask Jesus.

John, in Revelation 20, calls it fire from heaven and says that earth and heaven fled away.

In Revelation 14, the third angel warns of fire and brimstone and of smoke that ascends for ever and ever.

Malachi likens the final fire to an oven and the wicked to stubble burning in the stubble field. The saved will walk on the ashes (see Malachi 4:1, 3).

In Matthew 25:41, Jesus speaks of "everlasting fire, prepared for the devil and his angels."

Paul warned that sinners are killed by Jesus' "brightness" (2 Thessalonians 2:8).

God told Moses, "There shall no man see me, and live" (Exodus 33:20).

Peter wrote, "The heavens and the earth . . . [are] reserved unto fire against the day of judgment." "The heavens shall pass away with a great noise, and the elements shall melt with fervent heat, the earth also and the works that are therein shall be burned up. . . . All these things shall be dissolved" (2 Peter 3:7, 10, 11).

Ezekiel warned Satan that God would "bring forth a fire

from the midst of thee, it shall devour thee, and . . . bring thee to ashes" (Ezekiel 28:18).

Putting all these descriptions together, we have a fire that comes down from heaven yet is brought from the midst of Satan. It is likened to burning sulfur, which burns quietly, yet it makes a great noise. It reaches the temperature of a hot oven, but it consumes heaven and earth and melts the elements, all of which require much greater heat.

Apparently we are looking at something that cannot be described in ordinary human language—like transparent gold and glass mingled with fire. The descriptions are all genuine and valid and accurate, and when we see the fire, we will understand why it was described in all these various ways.

The medieval church looked at the texts we have listed and constructed an eternally burning hell complete with pitchforks and demons and a guidebook known as Dante's *Inferno.* Puritan divine Jonathan Edwards read some of the texts and preached a terrifying sermon, "Sinners in the Hands of an Angry God." Slowly, quietly, barely whispering at times, he warned his congregation in 1741: "The God that holds you over the pit of hell, much as one holds a spider, or some loathsome insect over the fire, abhors you, and is dreadfully provoked: his wrath towards you burns like fire."

Two and a half centuries later, Adventists abhor both interpretations as out of harmony with the character of God. We know that God doesn't have to kill sinners any more than a doctor kills a cancer patient. Cancer kills the patient; sin kills the sinner.

Someone has suggested that at the end of the millennium God simply lets sin play out the full length of its course. From the beginning of the great controversy, Satan has insisted that the universe would be better off without God's laws.

Following this line of reasoning, God could simply withdraw His control over the physical aspect of our world. He could tell the neutrons and protons and positrons and mu-mesons and antilambda particles and anti-xi-zero particles and the thirty or more additional subatomic particles that make up the matter of our planet, to go their own way and do their own thing.

If we understand nuclear bombs correctly, this sudden lawlessness among the minute particles of matter would result in an explosion so enormous it would make the blasts that demolished Hiroshima and Nagasaki look like mere sparks. In minutes, the world would be hotter than the sun. Everything on it and in it would dissolve, even vaporize, as Peter suggests. In this state of invisible vapor, the world would appear to "flee away." As clouds and mountaintops exploded, fire would appear to come down from heaven. And as sinners disintegrated, the fire would appear to leap up from within their bodies.

Satan would linger much longer than others because the body he has abused, leading billions into sin, was specially built by God to stand in His presence, in the full light of His glory, for a hundred billion years and more.

Whether this is really what the final fire will be like, we'll have to be there to ask Jesus. One beauty of this explanation is that it removes every trace of vindictiveness from God's part in the destruction of sinners. Up till now, He has refused Satan's demand that His laws be done away with. He alone knew the dire results of granting Satan's wish, and that's why He delayed. But now, in fairness to His enemy, He removes the restraints and lets Satan and sinners have what they asked for.

And the watching universe, who have already seen the degradation of character that results from breaking God's moral laws, now see in one frightening display of awesome destruction why God's physical laws are so necessary.

How much those who are outside the city will wish for a refuge in that holocaust! How fortunate we are! We still have time, with God's help, to bring our lives into harmony with His will. Then the protective walls of Christ's goodness will be our safe refuge from the all-consuming fire.

Chapter 14

"Come! Come! Come!"

(Revelation 21:1–22:21)

The Spirit and the bride say, Come. And let him that heareth say, Come. And let him that is athirst come. And whosoever will, let him take the water of life freely. Revelation 22:17.

The fire burns itself out. The ashes cool. Though sin and sinners are no more, the earth appears desolate and deserted, without plants or trees or grass. John, imprisoned on Patmos by the encircling Mediterranean, notes in particular that there are no seas.

During the holocaust, New Jerusalem seemed at times to be engulfed in flames and at other times floating on nothing. Now it is firmly established on a broad, barren plain.

Is there a flourish of trumpets, a stirring rendition by the heavenly band? John doesn't say. But presently he hears a great voice speaking from heaven: "Behold, the tabernacle of God is with men, and he will dwell with them, and they shall be his people, and God himself shall be with them, and be their God. And God shall wipe away all tears from their eyes; and there shall be no more death, neither sorrow, nor crying, neither shall there be any more pain: for the former things are passed away" (Revelation 21:3, 4).

Then John hears God Himself speaking. The persecuted apostle tells us, "He that sat upon the throne said, Behold, I make all things new." Lest any should question this statement, God speaks directly to John, "Write: for these words are true and faithful" (Revelation 21:5).*

John watches with mounting interest. There's excitement in the air. He sees some of the redeemed fly to the top of the city's wall. Presently more join them, and still more, finding positions where they can observe the surrounding country. Something very wonderful is about to happen.**

John studies the happy people on the wall. How different they are today, compared to their condition during those harrowing months in the mountains and dungeons, when pain and anxiety strained every feature. And they will always be this happy. The heavenly voice said so just now! The old days of sadness, the long nights of anguish are over. There will be tears no more. Death no more. Sad partings, no more. Pain and illness? *No more*! Only joy and happiness FOREVER!

John hears a choir singing a victorious song. Another choir joins it. Then other choirs answer till it seems the whole host of the redeemed are praising the Saviour for His wonderful works to the children of men. The top of the wall is crowded. Evidently, whatever is to happen is about to begin.

Look! Jesus is taking His place on His throne. He is about to speak! From His lips roll the commanding tones with which He created the world in the beginning. Before the delighted eyes of the watchers on the wall, the drab and barren countryside suddenly sparkles with lakes and rivers. Grass and flowers and stately trees clothe the rolling hills. Birds appear in tree branches, joining their songs to the hymns of the angels and the anthems of the redeemed. Fish leap in the waters; stately animals roam the woods and savannas. The earth is more beautiful than it was on that Friday afternoon so long ago when God proclaimed everything "very good." The

*The idea that the speaker here is the Father is based on Revelation 5:6, 7, in which the Lamb takes the sealed book from "him that sat upon the throne." Because the Lamb can only be Christ, it appears that in Revelation the One who sits on the throne is the Father (see Revelation 4:2, 3, 4, 10; 5:1).

**The Bible does not say the redeemed mount the city wall to watch the re-creation of the world, but Ellen White describes them doing so to watch the judgment of the wicked. Might they not do the same thing twice? (see *Early Writings*, pp. 293, 294).

gates of the city swing wide. At Jesus' invitation, the righteous press through, eager to inspect their inheritance.

No Temple There

After John saw New Jerusalem come down onto the earth, followed by the destruction of the wicked and the re-creation of the world, one of the angels that had helped pour out the seven last plagues took him, in vision, to the top of a high mountain and showed him a replay of the city descending.

From this angle, the city looked like a precious jewel in the distance, flashing against the black-velvet darkness of space. As it came closer, John saw walls of jasper, gates of pearl, streets of gold, and foundations of precious and semi-precious stones. Never had he seen a city so beautiful. Or so large! An angel measured it for him—1,650 miles around. Room enough for all the redeemed, to be sure!

One thing about the city struck John with special force. There was no temple. For a thousand years, the temple had been the main feature of old Jerusalem. Every vision God had given John here on Patmos had begun or ended in the heavenly temple. Surely there should be a temple in New Jerusalem!

But no. A temple wasn't needed anymore. For two reasons.

First, God had designed the heavenly temple to show the angels how He dealt with sinners on earth; and the much smaller copy of that temple, on earth, showed sinners how God dealt with them in heaven. Since sin and sinners were no more, there was no further need for the plan of salvation or of temples to help explain it.

Second, and in some ways much more significant, God had designed the earthly temple to be His home on earth so that He could live beside us. "Let them make me a sanctuary," He had said to Moses, "that I may dwell among them" (Exodus 25:8).

God didn't make Adam and Eve merely to inhabit the earth. He made them to be His friends. In the happy days before sin entered, He often visited with them. He hoped that as children came to Eden, He could get down on His knees and play with them, then take them on His lap and tell them stories, with their chubby arms around His neck and their sticky-wet kisses on His cheeks. As the children grew older, He looked forward to listening to them talk about the boy—or girl—they hoped to marry and about the great goals they hoped to accomplish with their lives. He looked forward to their inviting Him to pitch a few fast balls at their picnics, and to chatting with them as He stood in the food line at their pot-luck dinners.

Alas, sin spoiled all that. Most of Adam's descendants actually told Him to stay away. They didn't want Him in their homes. They didn't want Him playing with their children. Satan told Him the earth was forfeit and that He'd better not trespass. But God still yearned to be near His people. Over Satan's objections, He claimed a plot 75 feet by 150—scarcely as large as a building lot in a small town—and asked Moses to pitch a tent for Him on it.

Moses did, and later that simple structure became a magnificent temple; but the people became so proud of the walls and curtains, they completely forgot the One who lived in it. They made His home a den of thieves. When Jesus cleansed it, they crucified Him for interfering. God left them and turned to others. He impressed them to build churches where He could meet them. He told them that if only two or three came together, He would be there. Even if there were only one! "I dwell in the high and holy place," He told Isaiah, "with him also that is of a contrite and humble spirit" (Isaiah 57:15).

How much He wishes He lived next door to us, certainly no farther away than in one of the houses down our street. He would love to walk to our place in the early evening and knock on our door. (He's always careful about that; He never enters uninvited.) How He'd love to have us fling the door wide open and welcome Him in, then ask Him to stay for supper!

To be sure, Jesus will come to our homes today. But only by faith. Over there, however, in New Jerusalem, God's fondest wish will be fully realized. He will live on our street; certainly, He'll live in our town. He won't need a temple to meet us in. The whole city will be His, the whole country, and He will know He's welcome wherever He goes.

We mustn't be at all surprised, over there, when we're working with the flowers in the back yard, to hear the garden gate open and see Jesus walking in to chat with us, discuss our flowers and vegetables, and tell us how to get better results. Certainly we must expect, as we walk through the city, to see Jesus running races with the children up and down the golden streets or swimming with the youth in the river of life.

"Come! Come! Come!"

Because New Jerusalem will be such a desirable city to live in, we might expect the Mayor and city council to have a list of tough "restrictions and covenants" governing who may take up residence there.

And they do. "The fearful, and unbelieving, and the abominable, and murderers, and whoremongers, and sorcerers, and idolaters, and all liars" are specifically barred (Revelation 21:8). Because the gates will never be closed, thieves will not be permitted. Because children play freely in the streets, no child abuser will be granted residence privileges. Because the citizens will often be away, making new friends on distant stars, no jealous or immoral person will be issued a building permit lest, in the absence of husband or father, he might make improper advances to a wife or daughter. But why talk about these kinds of people? They will have been consumed in the cleansing fires that saw the end of sin. Yet we should think about them from time to time, because if we are like them, Jesus is willing and able to change us, providing we come to Him in time. And He's willing to change others who are like that, if we lead them to Him.

He wants us there. He'd love to have everyone there. Everyone He ever made. Everyone who was ever born. Everyone who has ever sinned. Everyone who has ever said he had no use for Him. He wants us all to come to Him now, while there is time, so He can make us fit to be citizens in the heavenly country and residents of its golden capital, New Jerusalem.

Jesus Himself said to John, "The Spirit and the bride say, Come."

To make sure that everyone hears the invitation, He asked all who hear it to pass it on. "Let him that heareth say, Come."

He extended the invitation to all who feel a need for the blessings New Jerusalem offers. "Let him that is athirst come."

Finally, to make sure that everyone knows that he or she is welcome, He asked John to quote Him: "Whosoever will, let him take the water of life freely" (Revelation 22:17).

There's that beautiful word, *whosoever*. Jesus used it when He told Nicodemus, "God so loved the world, that he gave his only begotten Son, that whosoever believeth in him should not perish, but have everlasting life" (John 3:16).

Everyone may be saved; no one need perish.

Everyone may come to Jesus and be fitted to drink the water of life.

The invitation is for you and me today. Dark clouds threaten our world. Fearful experiences lie ahead for both righteous and wicked. But the coming storm will not last forever. Someday, soon, it will be over. Blue skies and bright sunshine will yet again bathe the earth in beauty.

If we willingly accept Christ's threefold invitation, He will be much more than our refuge from the storm. He will provide us a marvelous mansion in New Jerusalem, around the corner from John's, down the street just a little way from His own. He'll visit us often, and we'll always feel welcome to visit Him.

Let's bow our heads and tell Him, "Thank You, Jesus. By Your grace, I'm coming to You now."